Reflections

from SHEPHERD'S GATE FARM

FOUR SEASONS OF
INTERACTIVE DEVOTIONS & COLORING ART

Reflections from SHEPHERD'S GATE FARM

DEBORAH HALL SUBETTO

ENCOURAGE
PUBLISHING
New Albany, Indiana

Printed in the United States of America

For worldwide distribution.

Library of Congress Control Number: 2023921229

Cataloging data:

Subetto, Deborah Hall

Reflections from Shepherd's Gate Farm: Four Seasons of Interactive Devotions and Coloring Art

1. The Christian Life (Religion—Philosophy) 2. Christian Living—Spiritual growth 3. Christian Living—Personal growth 7. Christian Living—Women's issues

Dewey decimal classification: 242.3: Seasonal devotions; 248.46: Christian life; personal spiritual practice

Illustration by Deborah Hall Subetto
Cover and interior design by Karol Bailey
Edited by Leslie Turner

Unless otherwise noted, Scripture quotations are taken from Holy Bible, New Living Translation (NLT), copyright © 1996, 2004, 2015 by Tyndale House Foundation. Used by permission of Tyndale House Ministries, Carol Stream, Illinois 60188. All rights reserved.

Scripture quotations marked (ESV) are taken from the Holy Bible, English Standard Version, ESV® Text Edition® (2016), copyright © 2001 by Crossway Bibles, a publishing ministry of Good News Publishers. Used by permission. All rights reserved.

Scripture quotations marked (KJV) are taken from the Holy Bible King James Version, published 1604, in the public domain.

Scripture quotations marked (NASB) are taken from the New American Standard Bible ®, Copyright © 1960, 1971, 1977, 1995 by The Lockman Foundation. All rights reserved.

Scripture quotations marked (NIV) are taken from the Holy Bible, New International Version ®, NIV® Copyright © 1973, 1978, 1984, 2011 by Biblica, Inc. ® Used by permission. All rights reserved worldwide. The "NIV" and "New International Version" are trademarks registered in the United States Patent and Trademark Office by Biblica, Inc.®

ISBN 978-1-960166-07-4 (paperback)
ISBN 978-1-960166-08-1 (hardcover keepsake edition)

Published by:
Encourage Publishing, New Albany, Indiana
www.encouragepublishing.com

GATHER YOUR BIBLE AND SOME FUN
COLORING AND WRITING SUPPLIES;
FIND A COZY, QUIET SPOT AND QUEUE UP THIS PLAYLIST.
THIS TIME IS JUST FOR YOU.

❧ • CONTENTS • ❧

A friend recently traveled on a mission trip to Zambia on the continent of Africa and related this story:

A missionary from the host country met with their small, jet-lagged but eager young team. The missionary was collecting information to match needs in the field with skills among the traveling team. He asked, "Who can sing?" A young woman in the group raised her hand and acknowledged that she liked to sing. "Good," said the host. "You are our worship leader." The young woman immediately protested, "Oh, no, I'm not *that* good." The host responded, "Well, it's a good thing we are not worshiping you." The group responded with silence, meditating on the correction.

Who do we worship? What has our attention? How are we using our time, talent, and resources? If we are consumed with our own glory, building our own platforms, or financing our own dreams, then we are missing the point.

"It's a good thing we are not worshiping you" rings in my ears.

Our God of miracles does not require perfect people to do His mighty work. He needs people who are willing to seek Him first. Are you ready to do that—together?

Here we go.

Winter

AS GOD'S CREATION IS TUCKED QUIETLY UNDER THE BLANKET

OF DORMANCY, EVERYTHING AT THE FARM SLOWS DOWN.

I ABSORB THE MEASURED PACE THAT INVITES ME TO LINGER.

WINTER IS A WONDERFUL TIME FOR THOUGHTFUL REFLECTION.

———————

1

⇜ · ABIDE IN DIVINE LOVE · ⇝

CONTEXT: *John 15: 1-17*

"YES, I AM THE VINE, YOU ARE THE BRANCHES.
JOHN 15:5A

———————

NEW YEAR'S EVE dinner settles in our full bellies. The fireplace sends warmth and a delightful yellow-orange glow into the dining room. The meal is over, but no one leaves. Holidays bring our family to the perfectly practical, Colonial "keeping room"— that wonderful gathering place in front of a fire and around a table. I am so thankful for the easy flow of conversation, the playful banter, and precious extra time to stay.

In our house, games follow feasts—games that often go on long into the night. Cards are dealt and strategies determined. Hope peaks with a win in sight, only to be dashed among the groans of regretful seating arrangements with an irritating discard. Feigned disgust and mumbles over "Who dealt this mess?!" and "Who is holding my card?" are tossed in jest with each round.

Eventually, we put the deck of cards back in the box. Tonight a dozen rounds of "Sevens" reveals that "slow and steady" still wins the race as I earn an unexpected win—by one slim point—after rounds of consistent losses.

It's not the winning or losing that matters—it's the *staying*. Surrounded by the most important people in my world—even for a few hours—I revel in the cherished staying of family. No matter how busy our daily routines, or how far divided by miles or opinions, we *stay* in the hearts and minds of our dear ones.

There are some missing—some empty seats at the table this holiday—yet, even they stay, as if embraced by the soft, tender wing of a mother bird, loved beyond measure whether present or absent.

And *joy* overflows in my soul.

One of our favorite games involves giving a partner clues to a word or phrase. There are all kinds of rules about what you cannot say as you urge your partner to guess the target and score the point.

I look at the phrase in front of me. I am confident. Easy play, easy point.

My turn. "Two words. It's a game. First word is the opposite of cold." My partner answers correctly, "Hot."

"Yes!" I am smug now, even as the timer clicks faster.

"Second word is the vegetable that you pass quickly."

The pace of the timer speeds up. It will go off any second. *Click, click, click.*

My partner shouts his answer: "Asparagus! HOT ASPARAGUS!"

Ding, goes the timer.

There is an imperceptible pause in the universe. I look with disbelief at my teammate. "*Asparagus*? Who plays hot asparagus?"

The laughter starts and we all dissolve into a cacophony of hoots and giggles.

And *joy* overflows...

The staying of our family produces another story for the generations: *Remember the time..."hot asparagus"?*

There is beauty in remembering. *Staying kindles the remembering.*

Stay. Remain. Abide. Linger. Rest.

Jesus spoke of this. I turn the pages to John 15:1–11 and find the Greek verb, *meno* (to stay, to abide, to remain), ten times in the first ten verses of the chapter. Jesus instructed us to stay.

I soak in the repetition. Teachers repeat important messages. Do you see what I see? Five times, Jesus repeated the phrase "Remain in me." This is an imperative sentence. It is written as a command. Jesus provided clear instruction for what we are to do.

"REMAIN IN ME, AND I WILL REMAIN IN YOU."

JOHN 15:4

I write the sentence. The blue ink moves in circles, underlines, and arrows. I see it.

Look at it with me. Write the verse below or in your own journal.

Underline the first "remain." Now underline the second "remain." Circle "in me." Circle "in you." Draw an arched arrow from "I will" pointing to "in you." Now read it again with all your squiggles and doodles.

If I choose to *meno*, to stay, to abide (dwell), to remain in Christ (in a close, personal relationship with Him), He *will* remain in me. God's love reaches into the depths of our being and He offers to stay with us—in us—for eternity.

That would be enough for me, but the promise continues. Look at the next verse. When we choose to stay, He *will* work in us and through us for His good purposes.

"Yes, I am the vine; you are the branches. Those who remain in me, and I in them, will produce much *fruit*. For apart from me you can do nothing." John 15:5 (emphasis added)

In this dynamic, enduring, staying partnership, God develops our character, provides opportunities, inclines our passion, and gives us all we need to bear fruit for His glory.

So what is the fruit?

Blue ink circles "fruit," and I turn my Bible pages to the right. The fruit of the Spirit is in the letter to the Galatians. Galatians 5:22–23 says,

"BUT THE HOLY SPIRIT PRODUCES THIS KIND OF FRUIT IN OUR LIVES: LOVE, JOY, PEACE, PATIENCE, KINDNESS, GOODNESS, FAITHFULNESS, GENTLENESS AND SELF-CONTROL."

The point of bearing fruit is not to make me a "better person" (although that is a natural consequence of the

Spirit's work in us). The divine *point* is to reflect God's character—to reflect His glory in a way that draws me closer, and others nearer to Him.

When we are filled with God's love, we can't help but act on it. His love overflows in us and splashes onto others. His sacrifice becomes ours—and we love in word, in deed, in honest, loving, humble service to one another.

I am a Christ-follower. I follow Him. I stay near to Him. The Father-Son-Spirit continues to mold me from the inside, so that I'm more and more reflective of who *He* is. Love and joy and kindness flow in the form of helping, serving, and loving others. That is the fruit that grows from staying in Him. John 15:8 explains, "When you produce much fruit, you are my true disciples. This brings great glory to my Father."

Stay. Remain. Abide. This yields fruit—the kind of fruit that brings glory to God.

Come to His table. Gather in close and soak in His Presence. Rest with the Word.

"I HAVE TOLD YOU THESE THINGS SO THAT YOU WILL BE FILLED WITH MY JOY. YES, YOUR JOY WILL OVERFLOW!"

JOHN 15:11

As I linger just a moment more over these verses, it occurs to me that it is the soaking that yields the splashing. Thank You, Lord Jesus.

Reflections

Describe your "keeping room," the place you love to gather with family and friends. What makes it a place that everyone wants to stay?

What does it mean to you to stay, to "remain" or "abide," in Christ?

What overflows from your life because you are connected to the Vine, to Father-Son-Spirit?

What kind of changes can you make in your schedule or your heart (or your mind, will, or attitude) in order to live more fully connected to the Vine (to God)?

Listen to "Abide" while you linger in His presence.

Be honest about where you are today and ask God to lead you forward with goals for tomorrow. Take some time to color and date the next page. Add a branch to the vine illustration that represents you. Will you draw a new sprout, a full branch, or a fruit-laden branch?

2

❧ · HERE I AM · ❧

CONTEXT: *Genesis 22:1-14*

"GOD WILL PROVIDE." GENESIS 22:8

THERE IS SNOW in the forecast. I don't pretend to understand how difficult it is to predict the weather—but it must be very difficult because weather predictions seem to be wrong as often as they are right.

I breathe deeply as I carry hay from the barn to the pasture for the goats late in the afternoon. The sky is the color of the ash in the fireplace, a dull white-gray. The air feels weighted and looks thick enough to cut, acting like a blanket for sound. It is quiet. It *feels* like snow. I think the forecast is right this time.

My animals greet me at the gate. Fourteen noses sniffing the atmosphere. Fourteen sets of ears erect and alert. Fourteen tails wagging. I smile at my greeting committee. They smile back.

Jethro, our livestock guardian dog (LGD), weighs in at 150 pounds of fur and muscle. Twelve sweet, happy Nigerian dwarf goats plus one extra-large wether (neutered male goat) add another thousand pounds of fluff and stuff. But none of *these* make as much noise as five tiny, feathered, hungry Runner ducks! I am not even sure they are that hungry as much as they are that bossy. The ducks quack and honk and flap their wings. "It's going to snow," I tell them. "Are you ready for snow?"

Of course they are not ready for snow! They hate the snow. And I am the one who has to get them "ready."

All the animals get extra feed and clean water. The ducks get one last jump in the pool before I "put them to bed" (secure them in the pen). While I work, I repeat the only lines I know to the song "Let It Snow, Let It Snow, Let It Snow" to the only audience that tolerates my singing.

When the hay feeder is full, the heated water buckets are secure, and the animals are tucked in, I make my way back to the house. Caring for my animals makes me so happy. I feel the joy down to my toes. It is my privilege and my delight to keep them safe, secure, fed, and loved.

I meet their needs because I see their needs. I see their needs because I watch, listen, and love them. This is what God does for us. He is our Provider. He is Jehovah Jireh (Yahweh Yireh).

Caring for others gives us tiny glimpses of what God's provision is like. It's deeply personal. God does not provide like an automatic teller machine at a bank, spitting out a means to a superficial end. No, our God sees. He gazes on His beloved. He knows our needs and makes provision for them.

Sometimes we need an extra-long time-out, like a forty-year trek in the desert. Sometimes we need a short march around a wall for seven days to shift our perspective. Sometimes we just need to give Him our two fish and five loaves and watch Him work. He knows exactly what we need and when we need it—and then He stays with us through it.

Genesis chapter 22 records the very personal account of God asking Abraham to trust Him, and Abraham's inspiring response of unwavering faith. In this story, God instructed Abraham to bring his beloved son to a mountain and sacrifice him there as a burnt offering.

Wait, what? How is this a picture of God's love and provision? We find the answer in the depths of faith and in the beauty of a relationship with our Father God who persistently moves us toward revelation of who He is.

As I look at Genesis 22:1–14, my eyes rest on verse 1: "Here I am." I love that simple phrase. Samuel said it. Moses said it. Abraham said it. I want to say it. "Here I am."

I teach second graders on Wednesday nights at church. When I ask questions, all the students raise their hands. With arms stretched high, they shout, "Pick me! Pick me!" They do that even when they don't know the answer—because they want to be *seen*. They want to be affirmed. Here I am. Pick me. See me.

How precious it is to be seen, known, and loved.

God called Abraham by name and Abraham responded. Abraham didn't question his God-given instructions. He didn't negotiate or hesitate. According to Scripture, he did exactly as God directed. He took his son, the servants, and the wood, and he went up the mountain.

Abraham, knife in hand, was ready to obediently follow through with the sacrifice when the angel of God called his name. And again, Abraham replied, "Here I am."

When Abraham demonstrated his genuine, wholehearted faith in God, He opened Abraham's eyes to the provision. There! A ram caught in the thicket. The sacrificial ram was provided by God in response to Abraham's unwavering trust in God.

Intimate, trusting faith allows us to shout, "Here I am!" even when we don't know the answer, because we know that God sees us. He knows us. He cares for us. He makes a way. He provides the way.

"O LORD, YOU HAVE EXAMINED MY HEART AND KNOW EVERYTHING ABOUT ME. YOU KNOW WHEN I SIT DOWN OR STAND UP. YOU KNOW MY THOUGHTS EVEN WHEN I'M FAR AWAY. YOU SEE ME WHEN I TRAVEL

AND WHEN I REST AT HOME. YOU KNOW EVERYTHING I DO. YOU KNOW WHAT I AM GOING TO SAY EVEN BEFORE I SAY IT, LORD."

PSALM 139:1–4

In the morning, I wake to a blanket of pure white snow. I pull on my winter gear—my snow pants, boots, and hat. I hike the snowy trail to the pasture and pause at the gate. The sun slices through the snow-covered tree limbs. It's twenty-two degrees and windy, and although it looks like about four inches of snow fell overnight, it's hard to measure because the wind hasn't finished rearranging it yet.

There is only one tail wagging at the gate this morning. One mouthful of teeth smiling at me. Jethro loves the snow. He must be part polar bear. The rest of the crew are resting in a pile of soft hay, chewing their cud, content to stay put in their shelter. I make my way to the duck pen and open the door. The ducks quack from inside their house, "No, thank you. We are staying in today. Bring snacks."

They fill my love bucket. They make me smile. Is this how God looks at me? Does He smile down to His toes with love for me? I know He sees me. I believe that He wants to draw me near. So I lean in—"Here I am."

Reflections

Who (or what) gets your love and attention more than any other in this stage of your life? Who (or what) clips at the heels of your love and attention?

"Jireh" ("Yireh") means "to see *and* provide." Our God, Jehovah Jireh, sees and provides. How has He seen and provided for you this day or week? *NOTE: If it's hard to remember what God has done for you, start a journal to record His work in, through, and around you.*

Abraham demonstrated devoted obedience that flowed naturally from a relationship built on love and trust. Abraham's friendship with God was formed over a lifetime of mutual seeking, seeing, and responding. Abraham was not blindly obedient. God is not coldly ambivalent. Abraham's faith was based on his confident knowledge of God's character.

I find it so interesting that there is no Hebrew word that simply means "to obey." Hebrews use the word *shama*, which means "to hear and obey." The action of obedience flows directly from hearing and understanding.

When God calls your name these days, how do you respond? Do you know and trust God well enough to, like Abraham, respond with devoted obedience—to *shama* (hear and obey)—to say, "Here I am" without hesitation when He calls? Why or why not?

God's Word is true. What promise can you firmly hold on to that will encourage you to know and trust Him more every day?

3

❧ · OVERWHELMED BY LOVE · ❧

CONTEXT: *Psalm 91*

"HE WILL COVER YOU WITH HIS FEATHERS.
HE WILL SHELTER YOU WITH HIS WINGS.
HIS FAITHFUL PROMISES ARE YOUR ARMOR
AND PROTECTION." PSALM 91:4

IT'S JANUARY IN western Maryland. I'm under the covers in a very warm bed. I know I need to get up. The dogs are starting to whine and the fire needs to be stoked. But it's so cozy right here. I hesitate. I pull the blankets over my head to block out the peeping sunlight. A cold, wet snout pokes under the covers. Large, brown Labrador eyes melt my heart and I climb out from under the blankets.

I am motivated by love. The animals all depend on me. Not just the ones that sleep by my feet in front of the fire. My fur and feather ice balls outside need me too. It's nine degrees this morning. I pull on my brown, quilted, canvas bibs and adjust the straps. I step into snow boots and don the practical but unattractive matching brown coat. I choose a hat that covers my ears and the waterproof gloves for managing frozen water buckets.

Imagine a giant, walking gingerbread cookie. That is what I look like dressed in my winter gear as I make my way to the pasture. Maybe the animals smile at me because they agree I look ridiculous.

When my chores are done and my body is warm again from the activity, I find a place to sit with them. The animals find different locations to rest. Jethro, the mighty LGD, will rest in the shade (even in the winter) if he wants a nap, or on top of the hill if he wants to be on lookout. The goats follow the sunshine. They gather where the beams of light and warmth find the earth. The ducks seek wind blocks. They don't like the cold, but they avoid the wind more than anything.

I settle myself on the hay between the duck house and the run-in (a small, open barn). I set Poppy on my lap and take off my gloves. I hold Poppy's chilled, webbed feet between my warm hands. She tucks her slim, feathered head into my ugly brown coat. We sit.

In the quiet, warming my sweet, cold duck, I give thanks.

God is so good. I meditate on His goodness. This awesome and powerful, perfect God cares about small, insignificant, walking-gingerbread-cookie me. He gives me life and purpose. He refines my heart and spirit. He meets me and teaches me every day. No matter how many times I disappoint Him, He encourages me forward. Step by step, Spirit to spirit, He guides me in love to persevere. To stay. To commit to the God who commits to me. To love deeper and wider and truer than I knew how to the day before. He is amazing.

Into His goodness, into His loving care, into His unfailing grace, I press my greatest hurts. There are circumstances outside of my control that bring unimaginable emotional pain. It is the pain of loss that threatens to carve deep ruts into my heart and mind if I am not careful to give it over to Him daily.

Pain and loss endure in this ungodly world. But God is always bigger than our pain. He outweighs the pain with hope and love. I am so thankful that we are never alone in grief. God can love and heal and meet needs that we cannot when we let Him.

I hold a duck while He holds me. Poppy and I, both tenderly enveloped in arms of grace and mercy. In this stillness, I am aware of His protection and provision. There is always cause for thanksgiving. He makes sure that there are blessings along the way to sustain us when we struggle. He is love. He teaches me to love.

Poppy's feet are warm and she waddles off to join the others. I don't feel the cold anymore. I am overwhelmed by Love.

Reflections

You are loved and you are valued. You were made by God on purpose and with purpose. You never have to doubt His love for you. You are His masterpiece and His messenger!

If you struggle with your value or identity in Christ, you might be encouraged by Hosanna Wong's "I Have a New Name."

"Be still, and know that I am God!" Psalm 46:10

"Be still" is translated from the Hebrew verb, *Rapha*. Rapha means to let go, relax, fall limp. The NASB translation uses "cease striving."

Read the verse with all of those words together until you have a picture in your mind about how much God wants you to trust Him:

"BE STILL, LET GO, RELAX, CEASE STRIVING, AND KNOW THAT I AM GOD."

You may have deep hurts. What, or who, is your "comfort duck," your Poppy?

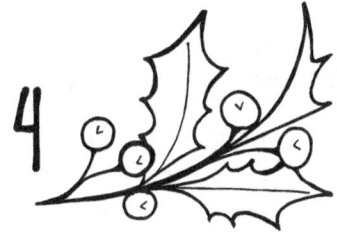

4

✿ • SALT OF THE EARTH • ✿

CONTEXT: *Matthew 5: 1-16*

"YOU ARE THE SALT OF THE EARTH.
BUT WHAT GOOD IS SALT IF IT HAS
LOST ITS FLAVOR?" MATTHEW 5:13

HAY IS THE staple of a goat's diet. They browse and nibble on fresh pasture grasses and plants. They enjoy fruit, veggie, and seed treats (my girls are especially fond of raisins and banana peels), but they require free access to nutritious, dry hay all day long to be healthy. Although many goat farmers choose to supplement goat diets with grain, what their precious little ruminant bodies really need is 90 to 100 percent alfalfa, timothy, or orchard grass hay—dried, cut, and served with love.

When you picture a bale of hay, you might think of the small, two-stringed bales that you put on your front porch with fall decorations, or that you sit on during a hay-ride at a local pumpkin farm. We don't use those. Our farm bales weigh eight hundred pounds and measure eight feet long by three feet wide by three feet high. One enormous bale feeds our herd for a month. We store ten or so bales in the barn to last from one harvest season to the next.

Once a day, I go to the barn with my hauling sled. I peel off layers of hay from the giant bales and deposit them on my sled. I pull the hay-laden sled to the pasture and fill

the hay feeders for my adored goats. Every day. No exceptions. They need this hay to live and to be healthy.

Today, when I peel the layers, the natural fibers don't separate like they usually do. I apply more effort. I pull, tug, and pull some more—until a layer of hay comes away from the bale. Instead of seeing green ribbons of health-giving sustenance, my eyes widen at the sight of ashen, molded, pungent, rotted chaff.

I work to pull away more layers. Dirt and mold spores waft in smoky tendrils around my face. I realize the rot goes through the rest of the bale. I move to the next bale. It looks normal on the outside—dry ribbons of green grass sprout from the top of each bale. I pull away the outer layer. It's rotten inside. It isn't edible.

One spiritual application might suggest 1 Samuel 16:7:

"MAN LOOKS ON THE OUTWARD APPEARANCE, BUT THE LORD LOOKS ON THE HEART." (ESV)

But that is not what the Spirit whispers in my ear. I gaze at the hay that is completely unusable for anything other than compost. My nose twitches from the rancid smell, and the Lord brings me to "salt."

When I finish my chores, I sit at the table and open my Bible. I look for verses about salt and find Matthew chapter 5. Immediately after Jesus explained the character traits of an authentic servant of God in the "Be-attitudes" (a compelling introduction), He taught about "salt and light."

"You are the salt of the earth. But if the salt loses its saltiness, how can it be made salty again? It is no longer good for anything, except to be thrown out and trampled underfoot." (Matthew 5:13 NIV)

I consider that word: "salt." He wants me to see. There is a string tied to the word that calls me to take hold and tug. I find another "salt" in the Scriptures—it is in Leviticus.

Leviticus may feel like a slow slog through archaic Old Testament rules and laws. But when we read this book through the filter of God's great love and perfect plan, His tapestry unfolds before us. The Holy Spirit illuminates grace-*full* threads, woven through generations since the beginning of time. He reveals more of His character and more of our chosen-ness. Look at this verse with me.

"SEASON ALL YOUR GRAIN OFFERINGS WITH SALT. DO NOT LEAVE THE SALT OF THE COVENANT OF YOUR GOD OUT OF YOUR GRAIN OFFERINGS; ADD SALT TO ALL YOUR OFFERINGS."

LEVITICUS 2:13 NIV

Moses brought the laws of sacrifice to God's covenant people so that they, by bringing a sin offering, could be forgiven and accepted by God. The "grain offering" in the Old Testament was an offering of the harvest to God. It foreshadows the life and service of Jesus Christ who completed His mission on earth for the glory of His Father, and offered Himself as the final sacrifice.

"NEVER FORGET TO ADD SALT TO YOUR GRAIN OFFERINGS."

LEVITICUS 2:13

Salt, the nutrient that seasons and preserves. Christ, the One who transforms and saves. Do you see the thread? I pull it again.

His life for mine. Jesus, the life-giving sacrifice that belays all other life-taking sacrifice, opens the gates of heaven for those who believe in Him. How should we respond?

Be the "salt." Live a life worthy of your calling and purpose (to love God and to love others). Live fully engaged as a witness to Jesus' love for you. "Salt" is our influence, our opportunity to show others how much God loves by how we, who say we love Him, choose to live.

I pull that thread one more time. God wants our offerings to contain the flavor-altering, life-preserving mineral, salt. Jesus said that we are the salt of the earth. This lost and confused world is watching. They need to see who God is by how we live. This is how we invite the lost in.

Sweet Winter Berries

Reflections

What do you have in your life that seems good on the outside, but on the inside is unhealthy, like rotted chaff?

What can you do today to start cleaning out the chaff?

Salt, used in the right amount, alters the flavor of something by drawing out the natural flavors already there. Too much salt is unpalatable. Too little salt is insufficient to change flavor. We don't want to be the seasoning that "leaves a bad taste" in someone's mouth about Christianity. How can we be the "seasoning" that others desire, helping them to lean in and trust the love of our heavenly Father?

In what creative ways could you be the "spice of life" and serve God faithfully by pursuing the calling He has given you for this time and place?

5

❧ · SNOW DAY · ❧

CONTEXT: *Psalm 23*

"THE LORD IS MY SHEPHERD;
I HAVE ALL THAT I NEED." PSALM 23:1

THE GENTLE, fluffy snow flurries that came in advance of the winter storm were just a tease. Freezing rain soon followed. Heavy snow fell between bouts of sleet throughout the night. The rising sun revealed a heavy layer of ice-crusted snow on every surface.

Awash in pure white frosting, the forest behind the pasture lures me away from the warmth and comfort of indoors. I love to hike in the snow. I follow deer trails in our back woods. I observe God's creation with my heart postured to His heart, my spirit inclined to His voice. This purposeful habit is not an emptying of mind but, rather, a filling of it as I quiet my soul, remember His Word, rehearse His promises, and count His blessings.

I place my foot in the hoof print left by a deer. I follow the animal's path through the brambles and thorns. I can move through places in these woods in winter that are inaccessible in spring when the underbrush is too thick to let me pass.

I see where a rabbit leapt. I see where a coyote pursued. The evidence is stamped in the ice-snow. I stay with the deer tracks until I find a place to stop and to sit.

Heavy snow changes the acoustics of the environment. Wind whistles through the tall trees, rocking heavy limbs. Dry boughs creek ominously under stress. Strong gusts encourage the snow-covered branches to toss their extra burdens. Snowballs fall from treetops with a muted *thump, thump* as they are instantly swallowed by the snow below.

The frosty chill of the air is a contrast to the heat that rises from my body with the effort of my hike. Cold exterior, warm interior. Ice on the outside, warm heart beating on the inside. In the quiet, He whispers. He reminds and I remember.

"HE HEALS THE BROKENHEARTED AND BANDAGES THEIR WOUNDS."

PSALM 147:3

YOU ARE JEHOVAH RAPHA, YAHWEH ROPHE, THE GOD WHO HEALS.

EXODUS 15:26

The Hebrew word *rapha* (or *rophe*) means to restore, to heal, to bind. God's character revealed in His name: "I AM the healer."

My heart pulses.

God will heal—when we let Him in.

The walls of ice we put up to guard our hearts only serve to keep Him at a distance. The harder we try to protect ourselves from pain, the more isolated we become. The Enemy is clever. We cannot let him win the battle for our heart and healing.

Jehovah Rapha stands ready. Freedom waits for you.

"'I WILL GIVE YOU BACK YOUR HEALTH AND HEAL YOUR WOUNDS,' SAYS THE LORD."

JEREMIAH 30:17

Wind whips my face. I know of the cold and the hurt that threatens to break me. I step through the frozen thicket, making my way back toward the house. A barbed vine catches the tender skin above my lip. The thorn draws blood. There is pain in exposure.

Exposure peeks into that tender place, opening wounds we don't want to reveal. And yet, those are the very things that allow His healing. Invite Him in. Confess your pain, your weakness, your insecurity, your doubt. Declare your mistake, your sin, your fault. Jehovah Rapha can handle it all.

Vulnerability grows the heart.

Being vulnerable means being humble and honest with God about everything He already knows about you. Vulnerability fuels our life-giving relationship, deepens our faith, and invites Him to do His work in us.

When those tender places are open to His perfect love, His balm transforms. Our ordinary human love is exchanged for God's supernatural love. We are healed to love deeper, to follow closer, and to become what He intended.

In this hushed, alabaster forest, I pray out loud: "I give You my shattered heart. I open my pain, my disappointment, and my grief to You, Jehovah Rapha, my Lord, my Healer. I invite You in."

I follow the deer trail to the clearing and into the pasture to finish my winter walk. I am in no hurry. I absolutely delight in time spent with Him. I am warmed by the light of His Word and comforted by His Presence. There is no greater peace than living with God's gift of grace. Thank You, precious Lord Jesus.

"THE LORD IS COMPASSIONATE AND MERCIFUL, SLOW TO GET ANGRY AND FILLED WITH UNFAILING LOVE."

PSALM 103:8

Reflections

Psalm 23 reminds us that God is truly all we need—in any circumstance. Read Psalm 23. Which verses speak to you today?

Jehovah Rapha has the power to heal all that is broken in us. He heals our bodies, minds, hearts, and spirits—when we let Him in. What do you need to confess to Him today?

How can vulnerability help you to grow and transform—to become more and more like Jesus in your own life?

Write Isaiah 40:31 here or in your journal. How does this verse give you hope through the healing process?

6

❧ · ON THE MOVE · ❧

CONTEXT: *Ephesians 4*

"THEREFORE I, A PRISONER FOR SERVING
THE LORD, BEG YOU TO LEAD A LIFE
WORTHY OF YOUR CALLING, FOR YOU HAVE
BEEN CALLED BY GOD." EPHESIANS 4:1

SINCE MY RELATIONSHIP with Jesus and my spiritual life go wherever I go, I thought I would take you along for my run today. As I was writing this devotional, I realized that the faster my body moves, the more scattered my mind is. This is not the slow, meditative, contemplative devotional—that comes later, with reflection. But not all of life offers quiet time. Sometimes, we are on the move. Even then—maybe especially then—we need to stay connected to God. So buckle up for this one; it's a bumpy ride.

In my fifth decade, I don't run as far or as fast as I used to, but it is still a thrill for me to be able to be outside, training my heart, lungs, and muscles while continuing my conversations with Jesus. My preferred route is a three-mile loop on the local canal. A canopy of tall trees on each side of the path provides ample shade in the summer. The dense stand of timber becomes a fortress against the strong, frosty winds in the winter. Several back-to-back storms dropped too much snow and ice on the canal recently, so today, I run on the plowed road instead.

I am navigating streets in a development, experiencing different forms of cold with each change of direction. Moving with the wind at my back and the sun on my face almost makes me forget the cold, but then I turn. I round the corner into a gust of wind. I tuck my chin and take the blast head on. The wind howls through my headgear.

I move my mind to scriptures as the effort to move my body increases.

I imagine my soft beanie as a helmet and push forward. I am a warrior wearing the helmet of salvation.

"TAKE THE HELMET OF SALVATION AND THE SWORD OF THE SPIRIT, WHICH IS THE WORD OF GOD."

EPHESIANS 6:17 NIV

The wind is fierce, but I am not even thinking of quitting. I will not be swayed by a little resistance. I will not be blown around by winds of change. In my imagination, I am battling the fierce wind that wants to move me off course. I grin at my own vision— does God giggle back, or is He rolling His eyes again?

"THEN WE WILL NO LONGER BE INFANTS, TOSSED BACK AND FORTH BY THE WAVES, AND BLOWN HERE AND THERE BY EVERY WIND OF TEACHING AND BY THE CUNNING AND CRAFTINESS OF PEOPLE IN THEIR DECEITFUL SCHEMING."

EPHESIANS 4:14 NIV

My runner's watch vibrates. A bright image shows on the watch face. It might be a pace notification or it might be a digital platitude such as "good job." I can't read it because I don't wear my reading glasses when I am running, but I look anyway.

Am I addicted to the constant flow of cybernated affirmation? Oh, Lord, help me to tune into what is important. Help me to tune *out* these meaningless distractions. This is my time with You. Keep me in the Light.

He keeps me in Ephesians.

"LIVE NO LONGER AS THE GENTILES DO, FOR THEY ARE HOPELESSLY CONFUSED."

EPHESIANS 4:17

"INSTEAD, LET THE SPIRIT RENEW YOUR THOUGHTS AND ATTITUDES. PUT ON YOUR NEW NATURE, CREATED TO BE LIKE GOD— TRULY RIGHTEOUS AND HOLY."

EPHESIANS 4:23-24

My thoughts are interrupted again, this time by pain.

My left calf resists the full weight of my striking leg. My stride shortens and my pace slows. I am limping and instantly irritated. I hate muscle cramps. I know I have to slow down or walk to save pulling the muscle. This isn't a race, but I want to finish, and I want to finish well. Paul finished his life—a fully focused life, a worthy-of-his-calling life—well. He wrote with confidence to his beloved Timothy:

"I HAVE FOUGHT THE GOOD FIGHT, I HAVE FINISHED THE RACE, I HAVE REMAINED FAITHFUL."

2 TIMOTHY 4:7

I wrestle a piece of ice from the snowbank and place it on my throbbing calf. I run it up and down my skin. The ice melts quickly against my skin and into my sock. The relief comes, the muscle is numb, and I can breathe easily.

My mind searches for the verse:

"SUFFERING PRODUCES ENDURANCE, AND ENDURANCE PRODUCES CHARACTER, AND CHARACTER PRODUCES HOPE."

ROMANS 5:3–4 ESV

I walk for a mile. I replace irritation with determination. I adjust my pace to run the last mile and finish the course. I am talking with Him, repeating verses in my head, and inviting His Spirit to point me to application while one foot falls in front of the other.

When I get home after my run, I look up the verses that He brought to mind. In three short miles, He reminded me of so many important messages. I meditate over them and let God's message speak over my life. I spend three days in Ephesians after this run.

This is my spirit working in union with His. This is my heart, continually searching the Scriptures for understanding and application. This is my life, in constant conversation with Him. And this is my purpose—to encourage you in your walk (or run) with Him.

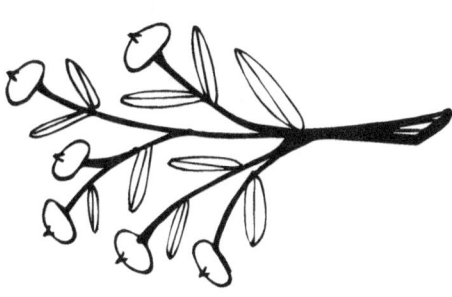

Reflections

How do you invest in your relationship with Jesus when you are "on the move," busy with work and life and obligations?

Though I couldn't perfectly recite every word of the Bible verses while I was running, I did look them up as soon as I got home. I am working to improve my Bible verse memorization. What works for you to memorize His Word?

Which Bible verse from this devotional moved your spirit today? Follow up with that one. Read the context around the verse and write out your thoughts and prayer.

holly

7

❧ · WONDERFULLY MADE · ❧

CONTEXT: *Psalm 139:1-15*

"O LORD, YOU HAVE EXAMINED MY HEART AND
KNOW EVERYTHING ABOUT ME." PSALM 139:1

LATE LAST SPRING, Runner duckling Clover made her debut as a fragile bundle of wet, yellow down feathers, gentle whistles, and high-pitched chirps. What a joy it was to meet the sweet hatchling just a few minutes old!

Clover grew quickly. She shed her baby feathers and soon blended in with her fawn and white flock. Like the other Runner ducks, Clover stood tall, walked quickly, and honked loudly. Mimicking the adult ducks, she learned how to forage for tasty bugs in the mud and the very important art of bill-rinsing in the tub after meals.

Runners (sometimes called Indian Runners) are a unique breed of duck shaped like a bowling pin. They stand upright with an average height of two feet. They have long, elegant necks, a narrow head, and a rounded lower body. They are excellent foragers and as such, they are often used instead of pesticides on organic farms and vineyards. Runners can swim, but these bottom-heavy, upright birds cannot fly.

My Runners do not trust the skies. Here in western Maryland, they are potential food for hawks, eagles, and owls. Our Runners make a habit of seeking shelter or moving closer to Jethro when large birds are circling overhead.

While the rest of my brood regard fliers with caution, Clover is drawn to the acrobats of the sky. She watches the fliers soar, dip, and glide. I watch her watching them. She angles her long, slender neck and tilts her head so her monocular vision is focused upward.

I linger in His Presence with my heart inclined toward His and my eyes on Clover. This is where I invite His Presence. Show me, Lord; quench this thirsty spirit.

Clover hops and honks. She stretches her small wings as far as they will go and starts to flap. She flaps harder and faster. She lifts a few inches off the ground, then lands hard on her webbed feet. She repeats this several times. With a final honk, Clover wiggles her tail feathers and joins her flock who have settled in napping spaces around the water bowl.

God made her a Runner, not a flier.

His Spirit whispers and I lean in.

Rather than longing for what I am not meant to be, God's Word tells me that He has a plan and purpose for my perfectly imperfect, unique self (Jeremiah 29:11). I can hold tightly to His promises. Why, then, do so many of us work so hard to be like someone else? Perhaps is it because we don't recognize our own value?

Have we confused the expectations of the world with those of our God?

If our eyes (really our hearts and minds) are focused on self rather than on God, we will wander. Clover's "eye focus" is "I-focus." This posture leads us away from His divine purpose.

Back inside, I turn those delightfully noisy, tissue-thin pages to some familiar verses.

I know that I am wonderfully made, so I start there. The psalmist is confident in God's work.

> ## "THANK YOU FOR MAKING ME SO WONDERFULLY COMPLEX! YOUR WORKMANSHIP IS MARVELOUS— HOW WELL I KNOW IT."
>
> PSALM 139:14

I can be confident in His work too. "Your workmanship" takes me to Ephesians.

> ## "FOR WE ARE GOD'S MASTERPIECE ["GOD'S HANDIWORK"(NIV)]. HE HAS CREATED US ANEW IN CHRIST JESUS, SO WE CAN DO THE GOOD THINGS HE PLANNED FOR US LONG AGO."
>
> EPHESIANS 2:10

I underline the last phrase and circle the first word ("so"). *So*—"and for this reason": "*So* we can do the good things he planned for us long ago."

He made us specifically, uncommonly, *on* purpose and *with* purpose. And He did that *so* each of His beloved would share their unique gifts in Christ until the gates of heaven are bursting with saved and maturing souls.

One more stop: Jeremiah 29. I want you to see something that I think is important. Jeremiah 29:11 is a popular verse. I've seen it on cards, digital platforms, and all types of Christian merchandise. But it's the verses that follow the promise that He draws me to today.

"'FOR I KNOW THE PLANS I HAVE FOR YOU' SAYS THE LORD. 'THEY ARE PLANS FOR GOOD AND NOT FOR DISASTER, TO GIVE YOU A FUTURE AND A HOPE. IN THOSE DAYS WHEN YOU PRAY, I WILL LISTEN. IF YOU LOOK FOR ME WHOLEHEARTEDLY, YOU WILL FIND ME.'"

JEREMIAH 29:11–13

There the spotlight falls. His plans for us include being in communion with Him. Oh, how He loves us! This is the relationship that matters. God in us and with us reveals His plans for us. His good plan includes salvation and a transformed life.

God listens to us when we pray and promises that we *will* find Him. When? When we seek Him with *all* our heart. God wants a sold-out, sealed heart.

God's Word tells the story. When we keep our eyes on Him, we get to live our best life—the life He planned for us. When we look to the distractions we lose our way. We wander.

He instructs me gently but surely through His Word. He tells me to focus on *His* heart instead of my own. Let Him fill me. Let Him be my all. So I say to you: eyes on Him, beloved—never mind those acrobats in the wind. He has something much better planned.

Reflections

Where do you feel like a misfit?

Consider the consequences of copying (imitating) others instead of being true to who God created you to be. Where could you have missed a God-given assignment while watching someone else live out his or hers? Have you left an empty space that your heart and hands were meant to fill?

If you truly believe that you are His masterpiece, designed on purpose with purpose, how does that belief guide your life?

Find and play "Come Thou Fount of Every Blessing" on your listening device. One of my favorite recordings is by Shane & Shane. Review these emphasized lines from the third verse of the hymn:

Let Thy goodness like a fetter
bind my wandering heart to Thee
Prone to wander, Lord I feel it,
prone to leave the God I love
Here's my heart, oh take and seal it,
seal it for Thy courts above

Spend some time with Him while the music plays. Ask God to help you surrender your heart to His. Write out your prayer here or in your journal.

8

❧ · CONTRARY TO THE WORLD · ❧

CONTEXT: *1 John 2*

"DO NOT LOVE THE WORLD NOR THE
THINGS IT OFFERS YOU." 1 JOHN 2:15

I lift the handle on the frost-free pump and water flows from the metal pipes. It drips over the side of the bucket, freezing as it falls, like tears captured midstream by the shutter of a photographer's lens. Motionless. Resolute. Set.

The dog-bear stands next to me while I work. This enormous, long-haired Anatolian shepherd has the look of a Saint Bernard and the heart of a warrior. I reach into the fluff and he turns his head to me. That giant head has soft, floppy ears and intelligent eyes.

I bend my fingers inside my gloves. The iced gloves crackle. The crystalline pattern pops and yields with the effort. I finish filling water buckets while Jethro waits patiently. When the buckets are full, I push the pump's heavy metal handle back down to stop the flow of water.

Chores done, we walk with the sound of crunchy snow under our feet. I notice that Jethro's paw prints in the snow are almost as big as my gloved hand. Together we climb the pasture's incline.

A lone picnic table at the top of the hill gives the watchman an unobstructed, 360-degree view of his modest kingdom inside the fence.

Jethro is our faithful working dog, our watchman on the wall. He is the guardian and protector of all the animals inside the pasture fence. He is huge and he is fierce. And he is fully committed to his assignment.

The goats run from him to clear his path when he is in pursuit of a potential threat. The ducks run to him when hawks and eagles circle overhead. Jethro has dispatched animals that don't belong inside the fence, but his impressive size and resonating bark usually intimidate predators from even trying to breach the boundary.

Jethro is more than mighty. He is also gentle and nurturing. He is innately aware that very small humans require gentleness. His entire body posture changes around toddlers.

When a goat or duck is wounded, he is the nurse who keeps them clean. But this 150-pound powerful, vigilant guardian is still eager for belly rubs and isn't ashamed to roll over like a puppy to present his great white belly to us for attention. He is our paradox.

A paradox, like Elohim, the God *all mighty*, the all-sufficient God who sought out Abraham, Isaac, and Jacob, also wants to walk and talk with me—and you.

Like Jesus, who taught us to love our enemies; that the first shall be last and the last shall be first; that leaders are to be servants; and that living requires dying.

Like Paul, who reminded us that grace is power, weakness is strength, and it is better to give than to receive.

It is no wonder that God's Word is foolishness to the world. These holy messages don't make any sense to an unbelieving soul. Oh, how gracious the Spirit is to reveal truth to us! This beautiful truth of how God teaches us to live and how to love.

We are called, chosen, set apart. This is important. My heart flutters with excitement as I recall the verses. We are a royal priesthood. We, His beloved believers, who understand His Word, are expected to live very differently than the world who does not understand. It is in living according to our calling that we *are* the light in darkness.

We are not called to fit in. We are called to stand out. God *in* us transforms us. God's Presence is the gift we get to share. It is no wonder that I feel I don't belong in our culture.

This is a revelation of the heart. I think about how often I have struggled to fit in, to be valued and affirmed by other people—but I have it all wrong, because it is a paradox. I am filled with joy—*joy* in His Presence. Joy in the miss-fit. Joy of not belonging to the world—because I am His.

Jethro rolls over in the snow for his belly rub. I oblige the gentle giant while I ponder all that our Father-Son-Spirit has done for me. I am thankful in His presence. I am thankful *for* His Presence. I have done nothing to deserve this open door, but I run in—and I am enveloped by His love and mercy, by His sweet, sweet Presence.

"FOR EVERYTHING COMES FROM HIM AND EXISTS BY HIS POWER AND IS INTENDED FOR HIS GLORY. ALL GLORY FOR HIM FOREVER! AMEN."

ROMANS 11:36

Reflections

What are you most thankful for today? Make a list and give Him praise.

God's way is increasingly counter to our culture. Do any of the paradoxes listed from the scriptures above challenge your heart, attitude, or behavior?

How do you live according to your faith, set apart from the way of the world?

What worldly distractions challenge you as you try to remain faithful to God's commands?

Confess any struggles and ask for His help. Write out your prayer. Don't forget to date it.

9

HOLDING STEADY

CONTEXT: *Psalm 73*

"YET I STILL BELONG TO YOU; YOU HOLD
MY RIGHT HAND. YOU GUIDE ME WITH
YOUR COUNSEL, LEADING ME TO A
GLORIOUS DESTINY." PSALM 73:23–24

———

SEVERAL INCHES OF snow and ice accumulated on the ground in January. The early days of February brought above-freezing temperatures and rain. The earth in the pasture is soft and beyond soggy this afternoon. I leap over the swollen stream with a splash landing. I sink into muck with each carefully placed step.

The goats don't go out in the rain. It's as though goats are made of sugar. If they go out in the rain, they will melt. That is my perspective anyway. A dozen goats refusing to leave a small barn for several rainy days creates another mess that I am sure you can imagine.

Shepherd turned king, David, knew all about soggy pastures, I suppose. He wrote:

"He lifted me out of the pit of despair, out of the mud and the mire. He set my feet on solid ground and steadied me as I walked along." Psalm 40:2

I move carefully, paying extra attention to my balance in the sludge, and I think on that verse. "He steadied me as I walked along." Both literal and figurative interpretations of that verse give me cause to smile as I work. I love the playful image in my mind of Jesus catching me before I slip into the slimy muck. Is He rolling His eyes at me, again? I grin for Him. He knows my silly side. He knows my heart too. I am so thankful that my heavenly Father continues to lead me through each stage of my life, from the unsteady spiritual toddler to a more emboldened, mature Christ-follower. He is so good.

> ## "HE HAS GIVEN ME A NEW SONG TO SING, A HYMN OF PRAISE TO OUR GOD. MANY WILL SEE WHAT HE HAS DONE AND BE AMAZED. THEY WILL PUT THEIR TRUST IN THE LORD."
>
> PSALM 40:3

I shovel, sweep, and clean the mess. This is not unusual in the spring—but it isn't spring. It is still very much winter. I check the weather app on my phone to peek ahead at the temperatures. We need a hard freeze or this mud will be impossible to navigate tomorrow.

I debate laying the "boardwalk" in the wettest areas. A farm boardwalk lacks a Ferris wheel, arcade, and soft-serve ice cream—but wouldn't that be awesome! No, our boardwalk is a simple, practical, "walk the plank" kind of path made by laying lumber over the mud. Nineteen degrees by morning. That should freeze the mud in place. I don't need the boardwalk—yet.

I hike back to the house to follow up on what God started in my head. I think about the steadiness of my foundation. It's not *what* I'm standing on but *who* I'm standing on that keeps me steady.

Sitting at the kitchen table, I turn to Psalm 73 in my NLT Study Bible. As I read through the verses, there are some that stand out to me—like that international signal flag that is Jethro's tail. I see my own weakness, my vulnerability—and I see His strength, His wisdom, and His way.

> ## "TRULY GOD IS GOOD TO ISRAEL, TO THOSE WHOSE HEARTS ARE PURE. BUT AS FOR ME, I ALMOST LOST MY FOOTING. MY FEET WERE SLIPPING, AND I WAS ALMOST GONE. FOR I ENVIED THE PROUD WHEN I

SAW THEM PROSPER DESPITE THEIR WICKEDNESS."

(VV. 1–3)

He reminds me how I can step straight into the mire of covetousness and pride. God doesn't promise that we will all be the same. In fact, I think He loves and values diversity. His creation reflects His great affection for variety. When I engage in the "sin of conformity" and pursue plans God intends for someone else, I miss the personal and divine assignment He has planned for me.

"THEN I REALIZED THAT MY HEART WAS BITTER, AND I WAS ALL TORN UP INSIDE."

(V. 21)

I write that verse in my journal.

I look up the original language.[1] The app tells me that the original Hebrew in this text begins with the conjunction "*ki*." This word can also be translated into English to mean "when," "then," or "because."

The word "heart" is translated from the Hebrew word *lebab*, which also means "mind" and "will." This Hebrew word speaks of the "inner man" (or, in my case, the "inner woman") and includes our thinking and inclination.

"I was torn up inside" is a modern translation of being "pierced," as the NASB says.

I allow the translations on my screen to linger in my mind.

---

1 https://biblehub.com is a free Internet resource I use often in my study time

Now I see a little more than I saw with my first reading. I understand that because my heart (and mind—my thinking) was embittered, I was pierced. I take my colored pen to the paper.

A bitter heart pierces our soul. My purple ink circles "bitter heart" and I draw an arrow to "all torn up." The verses preceding this one tell of the author's struggle with bitterness, the wrong thinking that leads him into a pit of frustration and confusion.

I put the pen down and talk to my God—my rock, my foundation, the One who keeps me steady. The One who keeps me out of the mud and sets my feet on a path that is good.

God convicts, challenges, and transforms my heart. He shifts my focus from my own selfish pride to His perfectly planned purpose. When I am self-centered, He gets my attention through spiritual conviction, and maybe an upset stomach (as I am "torn up inside").

Today He reminds me that there is no place for bitterness in the body of Christ. There is no healthy use of anger, jealousy, or pride in the family of believers. When/Because (*ki*) we yield our heart/mind/will (*lebab*) to God's Spirit, He will correct/support/steady us.

"MY FLESH AND MY HEART MAY FAIL, BUT GOD IS THE STRENGTH OF MY HEART AND MY PORTION FOREVER."

(V. 26 NASB)

I am full of thanks for this patient, ever-present God who stays with me, who molds me, and who encourages me every day. He gives me strength and balance as I abide in Him. *Who* I'm standing on keeps me steady. Any other source, any other focus, will lead me off the path and into the mire.

Reflections

Consider Psalm 73:3:
"For I envied the proud when I saw them prosper despite their wickedness."

Have you ever been in a situation where someone wronged you or hurt you and they "got away" with the injustice? I have. I learned a lot about myself when I was in this very situation.

God is patient and merciful with me—but He is just as patient and merciful with my "enemies." I remind myself of that when I am wounded. Can you think of a time when you were hurt and angry and wanted the source of that pain punished?

Can you see that person from God's view rather than your own? Do things look different from His perspective?

It helps me to think of anger and bitterness as a poison. The longer I allow those emotions to linger, the more damage they inflict to my body and soul. Those emotions disrupt and distract my relationship with God. Is there anyone or anything that causes you to struggle with anger?

Pray about the source of your anger—and give it wholly to God. Let Him deal with that source of pain so that you can remain healthy and focused on Him and His plan for you.

Write out a verse that reminds you to focus on God alone.

10

·❧ QUIET SONG ❧·

CONTEXT: *Ecclesiastes 3*

"A TIME TO BE QUIET AND A TIME
TO SPEAK." ECCLESIASTES 3:7

MORNING CHORES ARE done. The sun is rising, the sky is clear, and the air is crisp. Luna tilts her chin up to me and tugs at my heart with those beautiful amber eyes of hers. I can't resist. I reach down and pet her soft, ebony head. I'm not in a hurry, so I find a place to sit in the hay and Luna follows. She snuggles in next to me. She rests the bridge of her elegant Roman nose on my cheek. We both smile. I rub her neck and scratch her ears. I think she would sit here all day if I stayed in this spot.

The ducks are making a ruckus around the water bowl. They interrupt the peace with their boisterous quacks and honks. They don't like frost on their feet, and they let us all know about it. Five web-footed waterfowl jockey for position around the water bowl and then settle on their bellies, tucking their feet up under their wings. Once their feet are off the frozen ground, the quacking and flapping stops. Finally content, they are quiet again.

Luna looks up at me in the present stillness. This is her happy place. Maddie, Molly, and the babies are at the hay feeder nearby. The thermometer tells me the current temperature is 27 degrees, but as I rest in the barn with this snuggly girl, it may as well be sunny and 75. It is peaceful and all is well.

The farm has taught me the value of quiet. Quiet, I have learned, is not an absence of sound, but rather an intentional stillness that allows me to listen. As I sit here now, I hear the warbles and tweets of a variety of wild birds. I hear the goats munching dry grass. I hear the dog lapping water from the heated bucket. I hear chickens scratching the ground. I can even hear a wee barn mouse crack open a sunflower seed stolen from the feeder.

Anticipation stirs my soul in quietude. I close my eyes. I hush my mind and invite God's Word to penetrate this stubborn heart. I yearn for His Spirit to teach this eager mind. It is in the quiet that He leads me where I can't go in busy, noisy places. It is in the quiet that His magnificent light penetrates the darkness of mounting obligations and overambitious schedules.

"JESUS OFTEN WITHDREW TO LONELY PLACES AND PRAYED."

LUKE 5:16 NIV

In this verse, "lonely place" is translated from the original Greek word *eremos*, meaning uncultivated, an unpopulated place, freedom from disturbance.[2]

Eremos is also translated "desert" and "wilderness." Jesus sought quiet time alone—*eremos*—at different times and for different reasons during His ministry (Matthew 14:13; Mark 6:31; Luke 4:1).

Whatever the purpose of the location, it seems to me that the "freedom from disturbance" is the key. I can't hear His voice for guidance, for peace, for comfort, for instruction, over the noise that is my life. I need to be intentional about seeking Him in the quiet places. If He has something to say, I want to hear it, to see it, to receive it, to understand it. I need to be:

- *intentional—on or with purpose, making every effort.*

- *focused on seeking Him—seeking or searching according to His Word, by His Spirit.*

- *in quiet places. Eremos. Without disturbance.*

My Bible study and quiet time habits over my Christian life reveal a slow learning curve. I am forever grateful that we serve a patient God. I am grateful that He chooses to walk this tortuous journey with me, with each of us.

---

2 *Strong's Concordance*, s.v. "eremos," 2048.

This is a new season for me, a season that my whole being craves the quiet study of His precious Word. This "Martha" finally understands "Mary." More than anything else, I want to sit quietly at the feet of Jesus—and listen.

Jesus is always our model. If Jesus needed to take time to seek His Father in undisturbed settings, then so do I. Holy Spirit conviction leads me to relinquish my excuses for why I don't have time to sit still and to rest in His Word daily.

I abandon my excuses and He draws me in.

As I yield to the discipline of quiet mediation, He fills me up. There isn't anything more powerful than personal revelation of His Word. The Scriptures truly are His love song to each one of us. He sings over us with unconditional love and unfailing grace, like a divine aria to His beloved. This is a song you need to hear in the quiet.

Reflections

Let your mind be quiet while you listen to the song "Be Still and Know" by Steven Curtis Chapman.

If you find it difficult to schedule quiet time each day, what is it that challenges or interrupts this priority?

What can you change to allow for a daily time of quiet reflection?

When you pray (talk to God), do you also give yourself time to pause (wait quietly) to allow Him to respond, to lead you? What can you change to allow yourself more time to pause and wait for Him? The next time you pray, practice listening.

11

⤝ · FROSTY MORNINGS · ⤞

CONTEXT: *Psalm 139:16-24*

"SEARCH ME, O GOD, AND KNOW MY
HEART; TEST ME AND KNOW MY ANXIOUS
THOUGHTS…" PSALM 139:23

I OPEN THE door to another bitter cold morning and spy a thin, white canvas over the fields. From a distance, it looks like a soft blanket of snow. My feet know the way and my boots move toward the pasture gate. I see the sleepy winter grasses bent under the weight of…not snow, but a heavy frost. Rays of the rising sun reflect brightly on the sharp crystalline edges of the morning ice. Like glitter cast over a child's painting, the reflective bits sparkle and dance in the morning light.

I tend to my boisterous brood, stopping frequently to scratch behind ears and rub bellies. The animals (minus the ducks) never seem to mind the cold—but maybe that's what they think about me too. I spot a few runny noses this morning and add some fresh straw to the pile of bedding. I make sure the heated water buckets are secure before I make my way back to the house and the fire that will warm my toes.

The bright white frost makes me squint. The glistening light pierces my eyes—and my spirit yields. Instead of glitter, I see glass broken in a million tiny pieces. Reflective glass, a mirror with shards that break our outer layers. I slow my steps. I stop and listen.

The frost is beautiful, but not soft. A close examination reveals needles of ice, ridged edges, and sharp fragments of frozen vapors. I think again of a shattered mirror and I remember the verse from Psalm 139:

"SEE IF THERE IS ANY OFFENSIVE WAY IN ME, AND LEAD ME IN THE WAY EVERLASTING."

(V. 24 NIV)

Or, in my NLT Study Bible:

"POINT OUT ANYTHING IN ME THAT OFFENDS YOU, AND LEAD ME ALONG THE PATH OF EVERLASTING LIFE."

The ice holds my gaze; the verse holds my spirit and I offer a prayer. I ask God to show me what I need to see. I pray for a humble spirit to receive His instruction and courage to surrender to His answer. How many times have I resisted discipline because of my own pride? Am I blinded to my sin or weaknesses because I don't want to see it? I pray for forgiveness. I pray for His supernatural strength to be honest with Him and with myself. *Show me, Lord, show me my offense.*

I remove my gloves and reach out to the tiny, jagged crystals. I want the sharp edges to pierce my soul. Break through my outer layers of defensiveness. I touch the ice needle. It instantly becomes water on my flesh. Ice melts to water and trickles over my fingers. I take a breath and the Living Water pours into my heart.

I have sharp edges. I am surrounded by broken and jagged bits. We are all a broken mess. But God is not focused on our mess. He is focused on our redemption.

He claims and covers us, not for our striving or effort, but by His grace and love. He wants us home. God wants His chosen people to understand how very much we are loved and wanted. It's about redemption, not perfection.

The perfect love is His. When His Living Water flows from our hearts out of the fullness of His grace, we are right with Him. In our broken places, we experience His greatest blessings—we see that it isn't about us; it's always about Him.

Like earth and rocks worn smooth by flowing river waters, Jesus wears our sharp edges smooth over a lifetime of devotion to Him. And it does take a lifetime, not an instant. Revelation may come in a moment, but transformation is an ongoing process. Sanctification is not complete until we are with Him in heaven.

Keeping our eyes on Jesus, rather than on our broken pieces, is the path to transformation. God's plan from the beginning of time was for us to see His beloved Son, to let His Spirit do the refining work. The water on my fingers brings joy to my heart. I imagine that His heart is happy and He smiles at my understanding. I am His. I am loved. I am soaking in the Living Water.

Reflections

"ON THE LAST DAY OF THE FEAST, THE GREAT DAY, JESUS STOOD UP AND CRIED OUT, 'IF ANYONE THIRSTS, LET HIM COME TO ME AND DRINK. WHOEVER BELIEVES IN ME, AS THE SCRIPTURE HAS SAID, 'OUT OF HIS HEART WILL FLOW RIVERS OF LIVING WATER.'"

JOHN 7:37–38 ESV

How is Jesus "living water" to you?

What do you need to have flow from His Spirit to yours today?

Are you holding on to anything that impedes the flow of His grace to you? We are usually our own stumbling block. Give it over to Him today and embrace the fountain that will soak you!

12

✎ · A SLOW THAW · ❧

CONTEXT: *Philippians 3*

"I PRESS ON TO REACH THE END OF THE
RACE AND RECEIVE THE HEAVENLY PRIZE
FOR WHICH GOD, THROUGH JESUS CHRIST,
IS CALLING US." PHILIPPIANS 3:14

Ice

Ice hangs from the roof.

It sparkles in the sun.

As the day gets warmer,

the ice gets shorter.

And that's the way it's done.

TEN-YEAR-OLD me wrote that poem in elementary school. I recite it today and wonder why some things stick in our brains while other things seem to bounce right out!

It is the dazzling morning view of my ice-covered world that reminds me of the childhood poem. Every branch and blade is wrapped in a blanket of smooth, clear ice. Burdened by the heavy glaze, grasses and limbs stretch low as if in humble adoration to their Creator. My eyes remind my soul that, like these trees reaching for the ground,

one day every knee will bow (Romans 14:11) and all the earth will worship Jesus (Psalm 66:4). "How Great Thou Art" plays like a symphony in my mind. *Oh, dear Lord, how truly great You are.*

"LET THE FIELDS AND THEIR CROPS BURST OUT WITH JOY! LET THE TREES OF THE FOREST SING FOR JOY BEFORE THE LORD, FOR HE IS COMING!"

PSALM 96:12–13

It is late in February and I suspect this will be our last ice storm. Spring isn't far away. But meanwhile, we have an ice-crusted pasture and chilly goats waiting for breakfast. The hay sled glides effortlessly along the slick ground. The goats, always happy to greet their bed-and-breakfast patron, meet me at the gate. Counting tails, I see that I am missing one. Luna didn't come to the gate this cold morning.

Luna, our oldest, wisest goat, waits in the barn for her breakfast. As I fill the feeder, I watch her watching me. She isn't ready to give up her warm, comfy bed in the hay yet. So I join her. I stretch out next to my sweet Luna and rub her soft head. I share my thoughts with my girl while she sits, listening attentively.

The earth is turning and every day is one less day of winter. One less day of frigid temperatures, harsh arctic winds, snow, and ice. One day closer to the coming of spring, new growth, and its many beautiful shades of green. One day closer to the return of Jesus.

EVERY DAY IS ONE DAY CLOSER TO ENTERING HIS COURTS!

PSALM 100:4

It is the hope of His coming that gets me through the challenges of endings—and the cautious wonder of beginnings. It is the eternal perspective that wraps my heart, mind, and soul with peace in a season of uncertainty. It is His call, to know Him and make Him known, that motivates me to use my time well, no matter the circumstances.

Endings allow for beginnings. I am asking God for wisdom today as I have to let go, again. Releasing is often part of a healing process. Endings, leaving, letting go are losses often accompanied by pain.

But the pain of loss is different from the pain of regret. Loss is inevitable in this life—nothing stays the same. Regret is optional. Using our time, our moments, and our resources to serve God may include the pain of letting go—but it does not have to include the pain of "I wish I had done something more (or less or differently)."

Endings, like the slow thaw of winter, reveal tender ground and new possibilities. Soft ground allows the new seed to break through the dirt. A soft heart allows the Holy Spirit to transform a life. God does His best work with tender, humble hearts—hearts that are fully devoted to Him.

Endings are times for giving thanks. Thanks for the opportunity to experience the season. Thanks for the unknown blessings that new beginnings will bring. Thanks for the time to learn from what was given and to prepare for what is coming.

In this season, He is teaching me that full devotion to Him requires letting go of some things with which I have become comfortable. Full devotion to Father-Son-Spirit means coming to the end of myself.

Living God's way is not only counter to our culture, it is counter to our self-preserving, self-centered human nature. The ways of God are not natural; rather, they are supernatural. Forgiveness, love, and grace are supernatural. Trusting the unseen is supernatural. Living like Jesus is supernatural.

I lower my head to Luna's. Her fur is soft and her body is warm. I close my eyes and smell her fur, the fresh hay, and the crisp air. I hear rustling at the feeder, enthusiastic chewing, and a wild bird song in the distance. I breathe deeply and my lungs fill with clean, fresh air, reminding me that He is close and He is in control. I release the breath slowly and yield my life and this challenging season into His hands. *I am Yours.*

I hum the melody of "How Great Thou Art" in praise to the God who makes all things new.

Reflections

What do you enjoy about the change of seasons (literally and spiritually)?

What do you dislike about the change of seasons?

What challenges you when circumstances seem to be changing or are out of your control? How can you lean on God in these times?

List some things that make your life comfortable (relationships, dreams, possessions, routines, or something else).

Praise God for these, but also ask Him if there's something you need to let go of as you grow in Him.

Do you have new goals for new seasons (physical and spiritual)? Make a list on the following page or in your journal.

Spring

THE SEASON THAT YIELDS VISIONS OF BABIES AND BEGINNINGS,

SPLASHING IN THE RAIN, AND DIGGING IN THE DIRT.

THE HEAVINESS OF WINTER IS GONE AND ENERGY ABOUNDS.

EVERYTHING CHANGES ON THE FARM IN THE SPRING!

CAN YOU FEEL IT TOO?

SPRING MAYAPPLES, OH HOW I ADORE

ROWS OF TINY GREEN UMBRELLAS

STAND ALONG THE FOREST FLOOR!

SMOOTH, WHITE PETALS AND SWEET, LEMON FRUIT,

WIDE, VERDANT LEAVES TOP A WEE MOUSE

DREAMING SOUNDLY AT THE ROOT.

1

⇒ · THE GOD WHO SEES · ⇐

CONTEXT: *Genesis 16*

"THEREAFTER, HAGAR USED ANOTHER NAME TO REFER TO THE LORD, WHO HAD SPOKEN TO HER. SHE SAID, 'YOU ARE THE GOD WHO SEES ME.'" GENESIS 16:13

I'M FEELING MELANCHOLY this morning as I bear the weight of sad news. Sadness brings pain. Pain brings me to my knees. My hands wrap around my coffee cup in an effort to warm my bones this chilly spring morning. God's presence whispers and He brings me a gift.

The cat sees it too. We sit together with noses near the window. We are instantly captivated by God's spectacular imagination on display in the grass below. Two male Northern flickers are hunting in the yard for their breakfast. The spring ground is yielding a healthy meal. With gleeful enthusiasm, the birds pierce the damp soil with sharp, perfectly efficient bills. Their long, barbed tongues reach unsuspecting insects below the surface.

These birds shout to me of God's affection for uniqueness in His work. While humans seek to be common mimics of one another, God seems to prefer the uncommon.

This variety of woodpecker has a soft, gray head and warm, brown, perfectly round eyes, like a dove. Bright red feathers around the nape of his neck practically glow in contrast. Feathers the color of fresh cream give way to a solid black bib below his throat. A proud white chest sports black crescents and spots. Strong, sleek wing feathers parade brown and black tiger stripes like a tabby cat. The superior tail feathers resemble black and white zebra stripes, while the underside of the tail feathers are bright yellow.

All of this in one bird. The vision takes my breath away. What joy it is to behold such a marvelous creation.

God is in the details. He doesn't miss a thing. He sees it all, and He cares about what He sees. In Genesis 16, Hagar called God "El Roi." The name is translated from the Hebrew *El* which means "God" and *Roi*, which means "seeing, looking, gazing." "Roi" can also be translated "shepherd," one who spends most of his life watching (seeing) and caring for his flock.

El Roi is not only the God who sees—El Roi is the God who sees *me*. I ponder Hagar's story while I gaze on the wonder of God's incredible masterpiece on the other side of my window.

Some may consider Hagar's story to be a minor element within the larger story of Abraham and Sarah. I am convinced that even the small things matter to a God who is in all the details. So today, I am taking time to reflect on Hagar's experience with the "God who sees." Will you spend a few minutes with me in Genesis 16:1–16?

WE KNOW THAT GOD SPOKE TO ABRAM AND PROMISED HIM AS MANY DESCENDANTS AS THERE WERE STARS IN THE SKY.

GENESIS 15:5

But God did not provide for that promise immediately. There was a waiting period. A *long* waiting period. And in the waiting, Abram and his wife, Sarai, rushed God's plan.

We are introduced to Hagar as a means to an end. Sarai was seventy-five years old when she gave her slave, Hagar, to Abram (who was eighty-five!) so that Abram and Sarai could have children through the servant (Genesis 16:2).

Already, I am so sad for Hagar. In this period of history, slaves and servants were part of nearly every community. Hagar did what she was told, and, ultimately, she was used to achieve someone else's goal. I cannot even imagine a life like that. My spirit aches for Hagar. Her utter vulnerability pricks my heart.

When Hagar became pregnant (the very thing that Sarai hoped for), the relationship between slave and master deteriorated. Hagar ran away from Sarai's harsh treatment (v. 6).

I cannot know what Hagar felt at that time. I do know, however, what it feels like to be so deeply wounded that I want to be as far away from the pain as possible. Running away, alone and pregnant, was a reflection of Hagar's bereaved and desperate state of mind. Responses to pain often include efforts to escape or avoid the problem. If we are healthy, perhaps we will attempt to repair what is broken or to look for a chance to start anew. We have options in our pain, but as a slave, Hagar's options were very limited.

As a slave, she was practically invisible. She had no power, money, or status. Her value was based on her service. Where can a slave run? Who will help a slave? I can only assume that she was completely undone, overwhelmed, and afraid when she fled.

There is an important shift here in the story because Scripture says God "sees" Hagar. He sees "invisible," worthless, vulnerable, frightened Hagar—and He responds.

God sent an angel to speak with her (vv. 7–12). God gazed upon Hagar as an act of love and mercy. "El Roi"— God sees. He cares. He responds.

The angel told Hagar about her unborn son, even what to name him. Hagar was comforted. After the encounter, she referred to the Lord as "the God who sees me" (v. 13).

I imagine Hagar filling her lungs with the refreshing loving-kindness of a God who sees, acknowledges, values, and helps her. He wholly changed Hagar's perspective as His eyes rested on her.

El Roi is also the everlasting Father. The God who comforted Hagar several thousand years ago comforts me and you today.

"FOR YOUR KINGDOM IS AN EVERLASTING KINGDOM. YOU RULE THROUGHOUT ALL GENERATIONS. THE LORD ALWAYS KEEPS HIS PROMISES; HE IS GRACIOUS IN ALL HE DOES. THE LORD HELPS THE FALLEN AND LIFTS THOSE BENT BENEATH THEIR LOADS. THE LORD IS CLOSE TO ALL WHO CALL ON HIM, YES, TO ALL WHO CALL ON HIM IN TRUTH."

PSALM 145:13-14, 18

Like a shepherd tenderly guiding his beloved sheep, El Roi lifts His beloved out of the pit of despair and into His secure embrace. The same God who created every spot on every feather of the bird's wing sees every tear that slides down my cheek. I am not alone. He sees, He cares, and I am so very thankful.

Reflections

Read Psalm 145. Copy one verse that speaks to you from that psalm today.

Abram and Sarai interrupted God's plan with a plan of their own. Can you think of a time when you felt impatient in the waiting? Have you ever been tempted to twist or tamper with a God-given plan?

How did that turn out?

Hagar's response to pain was to run away. How do you typically react to the pain of rejection or helplessness? Is your typical reaction one that reflects your faith? Is this an area you would like to grow spiritually?

How does the truth that God sees you encourage you?

How does knowing that God sees *all* that you do motivate your daily choices?

While some people are impressed by "coincidences," I trust that God is in the details. Can you think of a time when God blessed you with a small thing that had a great impact?

2

❧ · SPRING RAIN · ❧

CONTEXT: *Psalm 28:6-9*

"I PRAY TO YOU, O LORD, MY ROCK." PSALM 28:1

SPRING IS MARCHING in with her grumpy pants on. Cold rain and strong winds have made an appearance every day this week. We experienced rain, thunder, hail, and a brief glimpse of sun yesterday. The creeks and rivers are rising. Temporary streams are forming in the pasture, giving the ducks extra hunting ground and the goats more places to avoid. I splash my way to the pasture each morning, careful not to slip and land in a muddy puddle.

Spring rains, like life's challenges, are both certain and unpredictable. Challenges are certain because we know, and Scripture confirms, "In this world you will have trouble" (John 16:33niv). The Word is clear. It isn't "might," "may," or "could" have trouble. We *will* have trouble in this life.

But trouble is also unpredictable. We don't know what the trouble will be or when trouble will arrive. We don't know the purpose or the consequences of the trouble.

Through my five-plus decades, God has taught me that "trouble" in this world always leads to opportunity. Difficult circumstances provide unique opportunities to grow our understanding of God, to strengthen our faith, and to mature our character. He has shown such tender mercy in my darkest times that I can honestly be thankful for the adversity. Working through difficulty and disappointment have ultimately brought His gentle whispers, His loving-kindness, and sometimes, even, joy—down to my toes.

In *The Problem of Pain*, C. S. Lewis said, "God whispers to us in our pleasures, but shouts in our pains."

With more practice than I may have asked for, God has taught me to bend my knee the instant trouble starts—to seek His strength, guidance, and purpose. God's Word tells me that God is love and His plan is good—so I can trust His plan, even when that includes wrestling with trouble.

I am so thankful that not only is our God one who sees ("El Roi") but also one who hears. God hears our cries and He responds (Jehovah Shammah). *That* alone is such a marvel. Our perfect, holy, mighty God, Creator of heaven and earth, hears my cry. The first words that escape my lips in prayer are, "Thank You, Lord." Thankfulness overwhelms my soul when I talk to Him—because He listens! A grateful heart repositions my spirit and makes a way for peace to enter in the midst of a storm.

His perfect peace, the peace that surpasses understanding, is the peace we need when we do not understand the plan. He gives that peace when we trust His plan anyway.

"AND THE PEACE OF GOD, WHICH TRANSCENDS ALL UNDERSTANDING, WILL GUARD YOUR HEARTS AND YOUR MINDS IN CHRIST JESUS."

PHILIPPIANS 4:7 NIV

When I trust God to work out what I cannot understand, my spirit is stilled like the water on a lake in the early evening—water so still that it looks like a sheet of glass. Not a ripple, not a wave, just perfect stillness. Perfect peace.

His timing is perfect and I do not need to advance the clock. Rather than hurry through or hunker down, I need to be obedient in the waiting, however long it takes. He knows what He is doing. How many amazing people of the faith saw death before they saw God's plan fulfilled? Faithful believers can close their eyes in sleep or in death trusting that God is still working the plan.

I don't focus on seeing the end (as in, "How is this going to turn out?") as much as I used to—maybe because, more often than not, one "end" is just another beginning, and I find myself in another cycle of blessings and challenges. The "end" is really when

Jesus places that crown on my head and says, "Welcome home, Beloved."

No matter what else trouble brings, it always brings me closer to Jesus.

Reflections

I have learned that asking "why?" is not always helpful. There are many things that God does or allows in our lives that we will not understand this side of heaven. A better question to ask in challenging seasons is "what?"

What, O Lord, do you want me to see/learn/do/change?

Can you think of something to apply this question to in your own life today?

Asking "what" can initiate a transformative response that carries us through the pain and equips us for the next season. In her book of the same title, Elisabeth Elliot said, "Suffering is never for nothing." So be brave and lean into it—ask what you can learn. Instead of gritting your teeth through the drama, invite God to transform your heart and mind as He grows your roots deep into the soil of His own heart.

I have heard many people say that experiencing hardship and pain allows them to be a comfort to another person, to offer empathy and meaningful support. I agree that is one way to use our experiences with pain, but keep in mind that God is interested in developing our character. He wants to mold us to be more and more like Him. The molding process requires a soft and tender spirit—one that has been crushed at least a little.

Do you trust Him enough to be putty in His hands today?

PSALM 28:6-9

"Praise the LORD! For he has heard my cry for mercy. The LORD is my strength and shield. I trust him with all my heart. He helps me, and my heart is filled with joy. I burst out in songs of thanksgiving. The LORD gives his people strength. He is a safe fortress for his anointed king. Save your people! Bless Israel, your special possession. Lead them like a shepherd, and carry them in your arms forever."

Journal Exercise

- **Use this page or use your own prayer journal to do this Scripture reflection exercise with me:**

  Turn to Psalm 28:6–9 in your Bible. I've also provided the New Living Translation on the previous page.

 COPY VERSE SIX.

- **Circle LORD.**

  "LORD," written in small capital letters in the Old Testament, refers to Yahweh. This is God's Hebrew name, so revered that Hebrew tradition was not to pronounce or spell out His name. Yahweh "LORD" is so much greater than "Lord" as master, ruler, or respected authority.

  Take a moment now and consider the complete and unrivaled holiness of His name.

- **Highlight "he has heard."**

  This is a gift! The holy God of the universe hears you. Just soak that in. Please don't take for granted that He hears and He cares for you.

NOW COPY VERSE SEVEN.

- **Circle LORD.**

- **Underline "strength."**
  The LORD (no one better) will support me, carry me.

- **Underline "shield."**
  The LORD (more than anyone else) will protect me.

- **Circle "all."**
  It is with complete, undivided, absolute confidence that I trust Him.

- **Put a box around "filled with joy."**
  That is what He does in us when we trust Him.

- **Draw a wiggly line under "burst out."**
  This is our natural, fervent, enthusiastic response to His work in us.
  We just can't help but give thanks and praise to Him!

COPY VERSE EIGHT.

- **Underline "his people."** His people are every believer, so that includes you and me. Thank You, God, for bringing us into Your precious family.

The "anointed king" in the psalm is the author, King David. It may also point to the King of kings, Jesus.

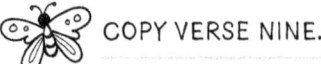 COPY VERSE NINE.

- **Draw a wiggly line under "your special possession."** The Hebrew word is *nachalah*,[3] which also translates as "inheritance." Believers in Jesus Christ are included in the inheritance.

- **Circle "Lead" and highlight "shepherd."** Some translations say "Be their shepherd." The Hebrew word is *raah*.[4] It means to pasture, tend, graze, feed.

This psalm of David ends with his shepherd's heart calling out to God to lead His people with tender care, wisdom, and counsel.

What circles, highlights, and underlines would you add to these verses today?

If you find yourself in one of those seasons where trouble has welcomed herself in, go to the Psalms. David understood the challenges of adversity. As a man after God's heart, he consistently poured it out to His heavenly Father. Father God, in turn, lifted David up every time. Find peace in His promises today. Lean into the arms of the Shepherd as He cares to hold you close.

If this is a season of abundance and peace, then hide these verses in your heart for the day that "trouble knocks"—because she will.

---

3   James Strong, , *The New Strong's Expanded Exhaustive Concordance of the Bible*, Red letter ed. (Nashville: Thomas Nelson, 2010), 5159.

4   Strong, *The New Strong's Expanded Exhaustive Concordance of the Bible*, 7462a.

3

❧ · PERSISTENCE OVER PERFECTION · ❧

CONTEXT: *John 12:20–26*

"NOT TO US, O LORD, NOT TO US, BUT TO YOUR NAME GIVE GLORY, FOR THE SAKE OF YOUR STEADFAST LOVE AND YOUR FAITHFULNESS!" PSALM 115:1 ESV

WE HAVE AN egg collection problem that requires a creative solution. The problem is that Jethro is collecting entirely too many duck eggs. His belly is evidence of his generous daily egg count. More eggs for Jethro's belly means less eggs for my belly. I am happy to share a few eggs now and then—but this is getting out of hand.

You may be aware that ducks lay their eggs on the ground, not in a convenient place such as the handy nest box inside a chicken coop, which is also, favorably enough, inaccessible to a 150-pound "egg eater." A practical fix would require our ducks to lay their eggs somewhere that I could access but our "Sir Eggs Benedict" could not.

With the wisdom of Solomon, my husband and I crafted a foolproof plan. We decided to enlarge and relocate the existing duck pen. We went to work to find the perfect site for the new and improved digs. We added a larger fence, secure gate, and a new, walk-in-sized duck house.

I managed the final additions of fresh straw bedding and a clean, full water bucket. We were ready to put our excellent plan into motion.

My non-duck-farmer readers may be wondering how we corral ducks from a large, open yard into a small, fenced pen. I move the ducks into the pen by walking slowly toward them with my arms stretched out to the side—making myself as large and as wide as possible. Now, if you don't know me, I am a healthy specimen of my French-Canadian heritage. All five-feet-zero inches of me on my skinny frame add up to just over one hundred pounds. To almost any creature other than a duck, I am not exactly intimidating. Thankfully, to these three-pound birds, I am enormous.

Our routine has been to close the ducks into their small pen at night. We let them out again in the morning so they have access to the full pasture and the full acre of foraging space. The ducks were very comfortable and cooperative with the familiar routine. Ducks are very good with routines. They like routines. We changed their routine...

The sun was setting and it was time to walk the ducks into their new pen and execute our fabulous egg-collection plan. I waved my arms gracefully like flags blowing in a gentle breeze and directed them into the pen. Well, one of them went in—the rest went around. I walked quickly to the other side of the pen to intercept the convoy. Walking slowly toward them again, I lifted my arms and aimed for the gate. One went in, and the rest went around.

I ran to the other side to redirect the flock of confused fowl. I waved my arms and turned them around—again. I encouraged them to notice that it was dark and bedtime. "Duck-ducks! Night-night!" They ran around the pen, again.

No more walking slowly; I was running now trying to keep ahead of them. I had them all lined up for the gate. I flapped my arms wildly and in they went—all except one.

Bravo wanted nothing to do with the new pen. I had to catch her and put her in. Finally, they were all tucked in for the night. A little more effort than I anticipated, but the morning would be easier. All I had to do was open the gate, walk in, and collect the prize eggs.

Morning arrived right on time. The sun was bright and so were my expectations. I stood outside the gate, looking into the duck pen. I saw where the ducks had made their nest and I opened the gate. Instead of running out of the pen as I expected, the ducks stood tall and still. They didn't move a muscle. Not a single webbed foot moved toward the gate.

I wondered what was wrong. I encouraged them to notice that the sun was up and they needed to get moving. "Good morning, my ducks! Time to play!"

They didn't move. Before I had a chance to decide what to do next, our smart, determined, ready-for-his-sunny-side-up-eggs Jethro (who can be surprisingly stealthy) moved in past me and made a beeline for the nest.

You can guess the next part.

Ugh.

You may be happy to know that with a little practice, we were able to establish a new routine with the ducks. We are currently collecting more duck eggs than Jethro. Persistence paid off in the end. Success!

The world defines (and redefines) success, and it is usually tied to perfection. "Perfect" is what the world wants, but "faithful" is what God wants. The difference matters.

Faithfulness to God and to His ways requires perseverance. It is the persistent and consistent effort that we make to seek His face and surrender to Him—over and over and over—that grows our faith and character. Faithfulness is a lifetime of surrender. Faithfulness to God mandates dying to self, not once with salvation, but daily. He shows me again (and again!) how completely opposite His ways are to the world's ways.

My sin-sick human heart is compelled to serve and honor "self." But I am called to die to self—to love and serve with humility. Jesus is not asking me to do what He has not already done for me. I think of His sacrifice. I pause and soak it in.

I open my Bible to John 12:20–26. I remember the context. These verses were written after "Palm Sunday" when Jesus entered Jerusalem for Passover and His "Last Supper." The disciple Andrew brought some Greeks meaning Gentiles) to meet Jesus, and Jesus spoke to them about His life and death.

VERSE 24 SAYS,

"I TELL YOU THE TRUTH, UNLESS A KERNEL OF WHEAT IS PLANTED IN THE SOIL AND DIES, IT REMAINS ALONE. BUT ITS DEATH WILL PRODUCE MANY NEW KERNELS—A PLENTIFUL HARVEST OF NEW LIVES."

The seed must be buried in the ground to grow into a plant. Seeds sitting on my windowsill will not grow. The seed buried in soil changes form; it transforms into the tender shoot and eventually into the full plant it was designed to be. Jesus is explaining that He must be buried in order to usher in the new life that will come with His transformation, His resurrection.

Jesus willingly gave up His life for me. Have I heard those words too many times? *Pierce my heart, Lord, not just my mind.* I close my eyes and remember. He literally, physically and painfully, surrendered His heart, soul, body, and spirit, a willing sacrifice to bear a punishment that He did not deserve. I have heard it said that the nails did not hold Jesus to the cross, but rather, love held Him there. I absolutely believe that.

My eyes rest on the next verse.

"THOSE WHO LOVE THEIR LIFE IN THIS WORLD WILL LOSE IT."

Jesus' death and resurrection threw open the gates of heaven. And what sacrifice do I make for Him? What life of gratitude do I live for One who gave all for me? *Help me, Father, to give up the self-serving attitudes of this small human heart. Help me to live with an eternal perspective and participate in the "plentiful harvest" that is the result of Christ living and working in me.*

This world is temporary. We can't cling to the small joys of this life as the ultimate prize. The "prize" is spending eternity with Father-Son-Spirit. Jesus taught, "My servants must be where I am" (v. 26). That is where I want to be!

I ask for Him to help me separate myself from the distractions and trappings of this world so that I can be fully present, fully available, fully aware, and fully engaged in the work He gives. This is how I follow Jesus; I am faithful.

Our Bible "heroes" (Abraham, Moses, David, Peter, Matthew, to name a few) were not examples of perfection. They stumbled. They fell. But they got up and pursued God and His commands for living, again and again. They were fully human, broken and affected by sin—as are we. They persevered through trial after trial and they didn't always get it right. But being perfect or right was never the point. Their holy mission was to point people to the faithfulness of God, not to the fullness of themselves. That is still our purpose today.

"BUT GROW IN THE GRACE AND KNOWLEDGE OF OUR LORD AND SAVIOR JESUS CHRIST. TO HIM BE THE GLORY, BOTH NOW AND TO THE DAY OF ETERNITY."

2 PETER 3:18

Reflections

We are challenged to stand firm in our faith, committed to God and to His ways in a culture that is consumed with self, celebrity, power, and money. Followers of Jesus do not follow the crowd. Followers of Jesus do not follow the current celebrity, the latest trend, or popular ambitions. Faithful followers of Jesus follow Jesus. Do you think this is difficult today? Why or why not?

Do you have a story to share about staying the course, being faithful over time and trials? Write it out on the next page or in your journal.

In one sentence, what does "die to self" mean to you? Do you consider this a daily process?

Do you have at least one person in your life who is a godly influence, a mentor, or wise counsel? How often do you get to interact with this person?

What can you do to be a godly influence and encourage someone younger in the faith? What name comes to mind?

What gives you strength to maintain your integrity and faith in the face of opposition? What wears you down?

4

CLASS TRIP

CONTEXT: *Mark 7:31-37*

"THEN JESUS CAME OVER AND
TOUCHED THEM. 'GET UP,' HE SAID.
'DON'T BE AFRAID.'" MATTHEW 17:7

———————

SPRING BRINGS WILD weather to our part of the country. The cloudy, cold, gray days of winter are finally in the rear-view mirror. The crazy weather eventually yields the flora and fauna that give rise to a general sense of optimism, the exuberance of renewal, the excitement of adorable baby everything (chicks, bunnies, and the like)—and lots of sneezing. This month all that sneezing led me to laryngitis.

I have never actually lost my voice completely before. This was a new level of inconvenience. My laryngitis coincided with a fourth-grade field trip to the farm. Twenty-four enthusiastic nine-year-olds, four adult volunteers, and their adventurous teacher arrived for an afternoon of farm lessons, animal visits, games, and stories. And I had no voice.

It was an absolutely gorgeous day and the students were very excited. I could do this. How hard could it be to get a large group of pre-adolescent children to sit still and listen carefully while I shared riveting information about the farm and the animals?

I know. What was I thinking? I was as crazy as the spring weather.

It took about ten seconds to realize that without my voice I had zero control over this situation. The first activity was actually a picnic lunch.

I know. How could I not control lunch?

Seating 101. Blankets were available for sitting at a ratio of about one blanket per three students. I gestured wildly for them to share the blankets and to sit close so they could hear me. These excited students grabbed blankets and attempted to set up their own personal forts and hideouts exactly as far as they could go. The teacher's whistle sounded and got their attention. A whistle! Why didn't I think of that?

Once they were all corralled back in the picnic area, they enjoyed their lunch while I strained my squeaky, ineffective voice as much as I could to get through the lesson. I ended with clear and simple instructions for what to do—and what not to do—during the animal-visiting time. Finally, I told them I needed a "head start" to move Jethro, our 150-pound Livestock Guardian Dog, into a holding pen. Their idea of a head start and mine were ridiculously different.

The boisterous group clipped my heels all the way to the pasture gate. To make a long story short, I don't think any of the students actually heard the "do *not*" parts of my instructions. Without a voice or even a whistle I was reduced to running around and tapping students on the shoulder to get their attention. They were so excited to be in the pasture with the animals that I had to physically touch them to communicate with them.

Later, when we lined up for games, I found that, again, I had to physically touch the children to get their attention. Their focus was all over the place and my pitifully weak voice could not overcome the volume of distractions. I maneuvered a few of the students like chess pieces on a board to help them line up for the relay games. There is more story to tell, but, overall, we had an amazing afternoon together and I would happily invite them back (after my voice recovers).

As I watched the final student climb into the last departing vehicle for the ride home, God reminded me of the power of touch. The magnificent, sweet power of His touch.

God spoke the world into existence. Jesus had the power to calm the storms, heal bodies, and raise the dead—with His voice. At His command, it would be so. But there were also times when Jesus chose to communicate by touch. He often healed by touch.

The children are gone. The pasture is quiet. The sun is warm. I sit on a blanket and turn to Mark 7:31–37. The scriptures tell us that the man Jesus healed was deaf and dumb (could not speak or had a speech impediment). As a retired speech therapist, I am very familiar with the communication challenges of hearing-impaired individuals. Maybe that's one reason this particular encounter is so meaningful to me. Jesus didn't speak to the deaf man (who couldn't hear Him). He didn't shout, or gesture, or do anything wild to get his attention. Jesus purposefully communicated His compassion with His touch.

Jesus touched the man's deaf ears. He touched the man's mute tongue. He didn't have to do that; He chose to do that. It was an incredibly loving gesture. With His touch, Jesus communicated that He understood the depth of this man's life-altering struggle to fully participate in his community because of his deficits. It was a personal, almost intimate touch, conveying Jesus' sympathetic heart: "I see you. I understand you and your pain."

Perhaps Jesus' touch communicated an even deeper human need—that of value and acceptance. Jesus reached out to the outcasts and misfits like no other. He was determined to share the truth of God's relentless pursuit for our hearts and souls with those who did not even feel accepted or worthy by their peers, let alone by God.

What a powerful and meaningful interaction! God humbled Himself to walk among us in human form, but He didn't stop there. He even chose ways to relate to those who were seen as "less than" because of their poverty, disease, or disability. With His touch, Jesus healed body, heart, and mind all at the same time.

A shout can be heard across a room; a conversation can be held across a table. But communicating by touch requires us to be in close physical proximity to one another. To give or receive physical touch means we must draw near, be vulnerable, and trust our communication partner. That's a tall order for some of us. But what a gift we give/receive when we draw near to God and to one another!

I ponder now how a gentle touch on a shoulder instantly captured a child's attention. Touch is a powerful communicator. We are not limited to fancy words or holy language; we can communicate love and attention with simple touches. In the appropriate context, a soft touch can express more than we can think of saying. When we don't know what to say, perhaps a simple touch says it all. *Thank You, Lord Jesus, for the healing power of touch.*

Reflections

What does close proximity and touch generally communicate to you?

Is it difficult for you to give or receive physical touch? What is your preferred means of communicating love and care?

I love that Jesus did not hesitate to be near and touch outcasts. The more I study the Word, the more I see God's heart for the minimalized, the poor, and the ordinary.

James 4:8 says, "Come close to God, and God will come close to you." What does that tell you about your relationship with God?

Can you think of a way that you can be an imitator of Christ in being near to the broken and despised?

5

❧ · FOLLOWING THE HIGHLIGHTS · ❧

CONTEXT *Jeremiah 1:4-8*

"WHEN WILL YOU STOP RUNNING?
WHEN WILL YOU STOP PANTING AFTER
OTHER GODS?" JEREMIAH 2:25

I OPENED MY Bible to the book of Jeremiah this morning. I am sitting on my deck with a cup of coffee on a humid spring Saturday morning. The dogs are at my feet and the wild birds are singing their morning songs. From my café table, I see Mama Wren tucked in her nest sheltering and nurturing her fragile eggs.

Words on the page penetrate my mind. Images form in my visual learner's brain as I picture the story unfolding. History running like a movie in my mind. His Spirit gets my attention. My eyes hover over the words. My heart beats faster. I reread and I understand. I feel His Presence in the beating of my heart and the changing of my breath. He reveals meaning like a splash of color on the black-and-white page.

This is how the Holy Spirit works. He illuminates and focuses our heart, mind, and spirit to see what God knows we can manage in this moment. In different moments and seasons of life, His revelation will also be different—for He knows exactly what we need and precisely what we can handle. He is so very faithful. He is always kind and so very good. I pause in my reading to give worship and thanks for the work that He does through His Word, through His Spirit.

Come with me through these pages and I will share what He highlighted for me today. I am praying that your heart responds as well. He has a word for you; pause and ask Him to open your ears and soften your spirit.

Begin by reading Jeremiah 1:4–8.

The Lord God, Yahweh, is speaking directly to a young man named Jeremiah. God told Jeremiah that he had been chosen to be a prophet, God's voice to the people. Jeremiah responded to the call with humility and honesty. I read insecurity between the lines. He argued that he was too young, but what I hear is, because of his youth (probably a teenager), he doubted his readiness, his ability to command respect. Was he wondering, "Who am I that someone older and wiser would believe or listen to what I have to say?" God acknowledged Jeremiah's fears and instantly aligned his perspective (vv. 7–8).

I am overwhelmed by the personal nature of our holy God.

God was speaking to Jeremiah.

God told Jeremiah that he was chosen, set apart, even while he was in his mother's womb.

God acknowledged Jeremiah's insecurity and comforted him with clear instructions.

God promised to rescue Jeremiah (which also implies that Jeremiah would require rescuing at some point in his ministry—also in 1:19).

Is your heart pounding with mine? Because of the blood of Jesus and the work of His Holy Spirit, our heavenly Father is doing these same things for you and me today! The book of Jeremiah, among other things, points to the new covenant—to our time when His law is written on people's hearts. What He did for Jeremiah six hundred years before Christ, He does for us today! And there is more. My eyes find verse 9.

"THEN THE LORD REACHED OUT AND TOUCHED MY MOUTH."

There it is again, that personal, intimate touch of God— the Father's loving-kindness that infuses a holy boldness within our own spirit. This isn't a magic trick, a transfer of power. This is a gesture of love. It is the proclamation of a Spirit-to-spirit connection that allows us to respond in love and obedience with divine confidence in Whose we are. God's touch. Wow.

I read a little more. Verse 10 gives Jeremiah an idea of where he is headed. The words are familiar to me, so I linger.

"SOME YOU MUST UPROOT AND TEAR DOWN...OTHERS YOU MUST BUILD UP AND PLANT."

Three hundred years before this, the wise King Solomon wrote the book of Ecclesiastes and addressed how history repeats itself. He wrote that there is "a time to tear down and a time to build up" (3:3). So here we are again, a point in history that is repeating itself. The chosen people were wandering from God.

I finish reading through Jeremiah chapter 2. As in the time of the Judges (more than one thousand years before Christ), when "all the people did whatever seemed right in their own eyes" (Judges 21:25), God's chosen people in Jeremiah's time had strayed from Him. "They followed worthless idols and became worthless themselves." (Jeremiah 2:5 NIV)

My highlighter bleeds over words on the page.

From verse 11: "my people have exchanged their glorious God for worthless idols." (NIV)

Verse 20: "Long ago I broke the yoke that oppressed you and tore away the chains of your slavery, but still you said, 'I will not serve you!'"

Verse 25: "But you said, 'It's no use! I love foreign gods, and I must go after them.'" (NIV)

The Jewish people were not living for the one true God (again). God and heaven's armies look with disbelief at a people who have exchanged the Living Water of a loving God for a broken well of their own creation. *Oh, Father, help my weak and fickle heart.* This is my profile, my story, too.

My highlighter rests on Jeremiah 3:12. I secure the cap.

"'FOR I AM FAITHFUL' DECLARES THE LORD." (NIV)

Abbey stirs at my feet. Abbey, my rescued cattle dog mix. This dog with a million irritating traits and one fabulous quality. This cattle dog's heart is absolutely loyal. She is as faithful as a dog gets. My heart pounds again. I look at the senior girl and she looks up at me. "All is well," she projects with her penetrating gaze, and "I'm here by your side."

With all of our irritating habits and room-to-grow spirits, our heavenly Father desires that we desire to be with Him as much as He wants to be with us. I close my study and pray a prayer of thanksgiving for a patient God who never tires of pursuing us; for a God who reaches out to touch us in ways that we can understand and draw near. *I just thank You, Jesus.*

Reflections

"The idols of nations are silver and gold, made by human hands. They have mouths, but cannot speak, eyes, but cannot see. They have ears, but cannot hear, nor is there breath in their mouths. Those who make them will be like them, and so will all those who trust in them." (Psalm 135:15–18 NIV)

What or who are your idols today?

The *Swindoll Study Bible*'s introduction to the book of Ezekiel says that God used exile (from Jerusalem to Babylon) "as a means to an end—to bring His people into a state of repentance and humility before Him. They (the Jews) had lived so long in sin and rebellion, confident in their own strength and that of the neighboring nations, that they needed God to remind them of His holy nature and their humble identity in a most dramatic way."[5]

We have this history penned by the Spirit of God, so we study it—so we can be different. But has anything changed? Are Christian authorities different from the Pharisees, or the Christian body different from the Israelites diminishing God and worshiping idols? How are they/we different?

---

5   Charles Swindoll, *The Swindoll Study Bible* (Carol Stream, IL: Tyndale House Publishing., 2017), 944.

I think about me "living in sin and rebellion," and me "living confident in my own strength." These stories are about God's pursuit and my need for repentance—daily repentance—because:

Like Eve, I have a taste for forbidden fruit and am willing to disregarding clear commands.

Like Sarai, I wants to solve problems my own way.

Like the Hebrews, I wander in pride-born circles around the promised land because I don't listen, or I don't trust.

Like Aaron, I am distracted by the crowds and by the "golden calf" in my hand.

Like Jonah, I stubbornly withhold love, waiting for justice.

Like Martha, I struggle with getting my priorities and my attitude in holy alignment.

Like Peter, I take my eyes off the Lord and sink into waves of doubt and self-pity.

God, change this stubborn, thorny heart. Transform this self-centered, myopic life. Touch my spirit to reflect Yours. Open this dull mind and allow me to understand.

Can you relate to any of my examples above? Which ones? Why?

Play and meditate on the song,
"Once and For All" by Lauren Daigle.

6

❧ · HOLY MOTIVATION · PART 1 · ❧

CONTEXT: *Zechariah 4*

"IT IS NOT BY FORCE NOR BY STRENGTH, BUT BY MY SPIRIT, SAYS THE LORD OF HEAVEN'S ARMIES. NOTHING, NOT EVEN A MIGHTY MOUNTAIN, WILL STAND IN ZERUBBABEL'S WAY." ZECHARIAH 4:6–7

NOTHING SAYS SPRING in our small town like Little League baseball. Travel with me, for a moment, from the farm into a favorite memory. The year that my oldest son, Jonathan, turned eight, he played recreational soccer in the fall and tried out for baseball in the spring. Jonathan is a firstborn. He was and is an achiever—never reckless or impulsive but cautious, thoughtful, and analytical. He is also very independent. He has always enjoyed doing as much as he is able, by himself and for himself.

Jonathan dressed himself on his first day of minor league baseball practice. He decided to don the athletic gear that still fit him from last season—including his soccer cleats and shin guards.

Before you judge me for letting my son go to baseball practice dressed for soccer, let me explain something. I probably did notice that he was wearing soccer cleats and shin guards to play baseball—but I didn't recognize it as a problem. I generally avoided sports that involved balls or sticks. I determinately shunned any games that involved people throwing or kicking any sort of hard object at me or to me. Not me; no way was

I taking a round for the team. I was not too proud to duck and run when the pop flies headed my way in gym class.

So, I brought Jonathan to his first-ever baseball practice—dressed for soccer.

I'm not sure exactly why it was such a big deal, but his coaches, Jonathan, and I still remember what he was wearing that first day of spring baseball practice twenty-five years ago. Jonathan was able to tell me the best part of this story. "Coach laughed initially, but during batting practice another kid hit a line drive that nailed me right in my shin, which made coach laugh again and say that he was glad I wore them."

I am happy to report that in spite of the initial wardrobe error, Jonathan managed to impress the coaches with his newly acquired baseball skills. And after just a few practices, the team put on their uniforms and stepped onto the field for their first game. Our fledgling baseball player was put on the pitcher's mound for the first game of the season.

The first batter came up to the plate. He was the same size as Jonathan, probably another eight-year-old. Jonathan took aim and pitched well. Pitch after pitch was good and he struck the first batter out. His coaches high-fived his teammates as they urged him on. I cheered from the bleachers, beaming with pride! What an unexpectedly fabulous beginning!

The second batter came to the plate. This boy was a twelve-year-old Goliath. Twice Jonathan's size, he cast an enormous shadow over home plate. I watched my son watch this boy take a warm-up swing. This giant-boy stepped up to the plate and Jonathan's posture changed instantly. Like a red flare launched into the sky, I saw what Jon saw. No one else saw it. But mama knew. This was trouble.

Jonathan stared at his immense target. I watched my son tuck his chin and take a deep breath. I was helpless watching from the bench. I could feel my child's anxiety. The confidence from his short-lived glory moment was gone. I knew that underneath his baseball cap, the tips of his ears were turning red and his neck was flushed.

Jonathan focused on his opponent. He was overwhelmed by the mountain he perceived in front of him. His analytical brain worked out the details and he lost his confidence. He was beaten before he threw the first pitch. Eight-year-old Jonathan drew deep, ragged breaths, and then, we all knew. This wasn't going to end well. Worry stole his joy and dismantled his courage.

Anxiety works that way, doesn't it? We *all* struggle with that uncomfortable feeling of doubt or uncertainty at some level, in some area. The discomfort of anxiety is lethal when it dismantles our ability to move forward, to take the next step, to make the next call, to throw the next pitch. Whether an irritating doubt, an insecure moment, or a

crippling fear, anxiety always minimizes our impact. Why? Because our focus is on what we believe *we* are capable of accomplishing.

God gives us hope and encouragement to face challenges that threaten to panic us into a useless puddle. In the Old Testament, God sent visions to His prophet Zechariah at a time when the Israelites were in desperate need of motivation and hope.

Two of my favorite encouraging verses come from the fourth chapter of Zechariah.

"'NOT BY MIGHT NOR BY POWER, BUT BY MY SPIRIT,' SAYS THE LORD ALMIGHTY"

(V. 6 NIV)

"DO NOT DESPISE THESE SMALL BEGINNINGS."

(V. 10)

Let's consider the context of the book of Zechariah. A weary and discouraged remnant of Israel returned to Jerusalem after being in captivity in Babylon for seventy years. This relatively small group of people was faced with the imposing responsibility of rebuilding a city and temple that lay in dust and ruin. Like Jonathan, they were standing on the pitcher's mound, completely intimidated by the enormity of the task at hand.

The almighty God knew that His people needed encouragement. God spoke through Zechariah, whose name means "Yahweh Remembers." God does *not* forget the details! Zechariah's visions assured the people that God would bless them and provide spiritual leadership to see them through the restoration of Jerusalem and the temple. In the context of a seemingly impossible job, the angel simply and confidently revealed, "It is not by force nor by strength, but by my Spirit, says the Lord" (Zechariah 4:6).

What does that mean?

First, we don't have to force the work or will of God. When we are engaged in the work He inspires, we follow or flow comfortably in the current of His Spirit. It's not a power struggle; it is a cooperative enterprise, a harmonious venture.

Secondly, our best human effort will not be enough to complete a godly work. When we work in our own flesh, motivated by pride or confident in our self-sufficiency, we may indeed complete an assignment. But, without the Spirit of God leading, guiding, or course-correcting, it is not a work of Him. Our efforts should always correspond with, align with, and be empowered by the Spirit of God for His purposes.

Thirdly, we do not give up and walk away from a mission inspired by God. God created you, chose you, and is developing you. He has plans for *you*. You honor Him when you trust and obey the call He has given you.

In Zechariah's time, God chose Joshua (high priest) and Zerubbabel (governor of Judah) to lead the people and this project. God's Spirit provided the motivation and inspiration. There were undoubtedly obstacles to face, but the angel assured Zechariah that God would level any mountain in the way (4:7). His leaders were chosen, anointed, and appointed—and nothing would stop this God-given assignment.

Reflections

Can you relate to Jonathan on the pitcher's mound? Have you ever been immobilized by insecurity, derailed by doubt, withdrawn in worry, and unable to move forward with a God-given assignment?

What dream is on hold?

What hope is deferred?

What plan is stuck?

What ministry is stale?

What relationship is stalled—because you don't have the confidence to take the first step, or the *next* step?

How do we stand firm on the pitcher's mound, face our adversary, and confidently yield to the Spirit of God?

Write out what you believe God is calling you to do that you have yet to finish—or begin. List the obstacles holding you back, and take some time to pray over them. Sometimes it's just not the right time. How will you know the time is right?

For we are God's handiwork

7

CONTEXT: *Zechariah 4*

"DO NOT DESPISE THESE SMALL BEGINNINGS,
FOR THE LORD REJOICES TO SEE THE
WORK BEGIN, TO SEE THE PLUMB LINE IN
ZERUBBABEL'S HAND." ZECHARIAH 4:10

LET'S RECAP FROM our previous time together: A group of Israelites was given permission to leave Babylon and return to Jerusalem to rebuild the temple of God. This small contingent bore the physical and emotional burden of rebuilding a once beautiful and elaborate holy temple. Make no mistake, this was an impossibly enormous task. The people were paralyzed by the weight of this responsibility. But God…

God provided encouragement and hope to the Israelites through the prophet Zechariah and the leader (or governor) of the people, Zerubbabel. He gave Zechariah visions that revealed God's favor and plan, and Zerubbabel followed the commands. In verse 10 of chapter 4, God provided the motivation to begin the process. "Do not despise these small beginnings, for the Lord rejoices to see the work begin, to see the plumb line in Zerubbabel's hand."

The small things, the tiny, precious first steps taken in faith and obedience, matter to our God—who is searching for those who are committed to Him and faithful to His work. Zechariah's vision pointed to 2 Chronicles 16:9: "For the eyes of the Lord range

throughout the earth to strengthen those whose hearts are fully committed to him" (niv).

God knows the ache of our heart. He knows our fear of failure and our hesitation in insecurity. He also knows that when our eyes are not focused and our hearts are not fully devoted to Him, we make room for the Enemy's lies to seep into our spirit. Read that previous sentence again; underline it. It's important.

When God gives us an assignment, the Enemy's ears are pricked. A distracted, divided heart is a target. Satan can't take a believer's soul, so the master deceiver works to limit our ministry and our effectiveness. The Enemy is crafty— we must not give him room to work in our mind and spirit. Our failure to step up or out when we are called reveals a heart that trusts the Enemy's lies over God's truth. We must be intentional about keeping our eyes on God to block the schemes of the liar.

The Lord surely *rejoices* in our faithful first attempts, in our beginnings. The smallest steps forward make God smile! Imagine God smiling and cheering you on as you make the smallest move forward in the direction He has called you. Every step is part of the sanctification process. Every step is an opportunity to learn, grow, and transform.

Read verse 10 one more time. It mentions the plumb line. What's that all about? A plumb line is a very simple but valuable tool. A plumb line is essentially a weight suspended from a string that is used during construction to ensure structural integrity. The vertical assessment (with a plumb line) allows the builder to determine whether or not the building is vertically centered, leaning left or right, in or out—and adjust as indicated.

Spiritually speaking, God's Word is our plumb line. God's Word and His ways are not subject to changes of opinion and culture. His moral law is true and steady. Christ-followers benefit from the practice of routine vertical assessments. A spiritual checkup, via a plumb line anchored in His Word, Spirit, and character, will boost your confidence when you wonder things like *Am I in God's will, pursuing His purpose, on the right track? Does this activity align with His commands?*

When God sees your alignment with Him, He rejoices! He *sees* and celebrates not only a finished product but also the faithful steps along the way! I don't want to minimize His role, but in some ways, God is your greatest cheerleader. The original Hebrew word in this scripture is *samach*.[6] It means cheers, gives joy, happiness, rejoice.

When we find ourselves overwhelmed, exhausted, uncertain of how to begin or where to start, we can be encouraged by God's position—He is cheering us on to take those first brave steps forward. He has a plan and it is good.

So back to baseball. That first game was not the end of baseball for Jonathan. That one stressful moment as an eight-year-old was a small step, a trepid beginning, rather than a traumatic ending. Jonathan was able to take one step at a time to mature and develop on a path that provided fabulous experiences and life lessons along the way. In fact, in the end, Jonathan loved and played baseball for more than a decade. He played well, formed lifelong relationships, and learned and thrived under several coaches. He played on All-Star teams and through high school and even a year in college.

Baseball brought my family so much joy throughout the years, along with opportunities to share the love of God with others who also loved the game. The next time you find yourself "stuck," grab your how-to manual—God's Word. You don't want to miss out on what He has planned for you!

---

6   James Strong, *The New Strong's Expanded Exhaustive Concordance of the Bible*, Red letter ed. (Nashville: Thomas Nelson, 2010), 8055.

Reflections

Do you have a large task to accomplish, something that feels overwhelming? What first steps toward your goal can you take today?

What kind of baby steps encourage you to begin and then to persevere through a difficult process?

I have been guilty of understanding a God-given assignment and then running on ahead because I think I know what I'm doing. This routine gets me in trouble because I often run right past God's plan and into my own. Small steps forward allow us to watch God work and to course-correct as we go along. Small steps forward keep us aligned with God and His purposes. Small steps also keep us humble—so we don't feel too full of ourselves in the end.

Can you relate to any of these ideas?

Do you tend to move slow and steady through a project, or are you a charge-ahead kind of person?

Consider the advantages and disadvantages of your God-given temperament and bents. How have you seen God use your unique strengths and/or weaknesses to complete assignments He has given you to impact others?

8

❧ · THE RESCUE · ❧

CONTEXT: *Psalm 18*

"HE LED ME TO A PLACE OF SAFETY; HE RESCUED
ME BECAUSE HE DELIGHTS IN ME." PSALM 18:19

AVA IS A YOUNG, thirty-pound love bug that arrived at our farm early this spring as a "foster" dog. She is a short-haired, mixed-breed stray who was rescued from death row at a shelter. Ava is an enthusiastic pup who wore her first foster mama out, making me foster mama number two. A sleek black coat, floppy lab ears, and alert, pug-like puppy eyes bounded out of the vehicle that arrived in our driveway. Ava's shelter name was Nova and we laughed as she shot around the yard and inside the fence like a supernova. Our heartstrings tangled up at first sight and she was my dog before I had a chance to say hello.

Ava had a difficult beginning. She lived on the streets, scavenged for food, and slept under cars. There was no fluffy dog bed, no pretty collar, and no faithful friend to stroke her head or love on her. She was malnourished and full of parasites.

Ava was deemed "unwanted," "undesirable," and "unadoptable" in a shelter that didn't have room for another animal, let alone a sick one. She was scheduled to be euthanized when a private rescue organization pulled her from the shelter and placed her in a foster home for her first stage of rehabilitation.

She was rescued. Every day there are dogs who are not pulled and given a second chance. Every day there are dogs lost to the system with no one to cry, to help or redeem them. I am so thankful for Jesus. He is the mighty God who saves! Even on my worst days, Jesus never considers me undesirable. He rescued me and secured my future.

Saved.

Secured.

Ransomed.

REDEEMED.

We don't use the word *redeemer* often. It doesn't roll off my tongue in casual conversation. Perhaps it should, for I am so very grateful for my sweet Redeemer, Jesus Christ—the One who pulled me from a shelter, so to speak, of my own self-centered making.

My greatest struggle with accepting Jesus as Lord and Savior as a young adult was, quite simply, that I did not believe I needed to be rescued. I considered myself to be a good person. I was an independent, highly motivated achiever. I had clear educational and career goals. I was strong, proud, and confident. I did not need "saving"—that was inconceivable to me.

How do you explain to a young, successful, confident, free-spirited woman that she needs to be rescued from her life of sin? You don't, really. The Holy Spirit does the work of convicting and claiming our hearts, transforming our lives, and putting us on a path to ever-expanding devotion to God.

God is persistent. English poet Francis Thompson called Him "the Hound of Heaven" for His relentless pursuit of a meaningful relationship with us. God's love pursues us at an unhurried pace. In hindsight, I can think of dozens of times He tried to get my attention during my youth. I ignored, rejected, or justified every divine outreach until I finally recognized that whisper, that prompt, that conviction was of the Holy Spirit.

But before He showed me my sin and weakness, He showed me His love. After I experienced His love, I was able to see His grace—and understand my depravity. For me, love came first. I could not see how bad I was until I experienced how good He is.

When the scales fell off my eyes, I saw that I was the dog in the cage. I was weak, unhealthy, limited, and on death row! I needed—I *wanted*—a Savior to lift me up, to break my chains, and to invite me into His family!

So now I am writing to my daughters, to my sisters, to my friends who may not know: You are so loved. Hear, my beloved, how very precious you are to Him, and to

His family. There is nothing, *no thing*, you have ever said, done, or thought that can deter His pursuit of you. The farther you wander, the louder He calls. He wants you home.

Hear, my beloved, that you are wanted. You are the desire of His heart and the treasure of His Spirit. He created you as His poetry—His masterpiece. He wants to complete you and to comfort you. He wants to grow you and to stretch you. He wants you to spend eternity with Him and our family. You can doubt yourself, but don't ever doubt the power and persistence of God's everlasting, unconditional, extravagant, infinite, perfect love and grace for you. He never gives up on you. Never.

He is the One who will lift your chin and look into your eyes and tell you that you are precious. He is the One who will set your path straight and align your heart with His. He is the One who will provide the acceptance you desire, the peace you crave, and the purpose that gives meaning to your life. He is the One who will rescue your soul from the torment of regret, anger, and pain. He is the One who replaces disappointment with delight as He delights in whose you are!

Ava got her second chance. You get a million do-overs if you need them. I am praying for you today. Lift your eyes to Him. Take His hand and rest your head on His heart. He wants that more than anything in the world.

"THE LORD YOUR GOD IS IN YOUR MIDST, A MIGHTY ONE WHO WILL SAVE; HE WILL REJOICE OVER YOU WITH GLADNESS; HE WILL QUIET YOU BY HIS LOVE; HE WILL EXULT OVER YOU WITH LOUD SINGING."

ZEPHANIAH 3:17 ESV

"BUT GOD, BEING RICH IN MERCY, BECAUSE OF THE GREAT LOVE WITH WHICH HE LOVED US, EVEN WHEN WE WERE DEAD IN OUR TRESPASSES, MADE US ALIVE TOGETHER WITH CHRIST—BY GRACE YOU HAVE BEEN SAVED. "

EPHESIANS 2:4–5 ESV

Reflections

Play or read the beautiful hymn, "I Will Sing of My Redeemer" by Philip P. Bliss (1876):

VERSE 1

I will sing of my Redeemer and His wondrous love to me;
On the cruel cross He suffered, from the curse to set me free.

Sing, oh sing, of my Redeemer, with His blood, He purchased me.
On the cross, He sealed my pardon, paid the debt, and made me free.

VERSE 2

I will tell the wondrous story, how my lost estate to save,
In His boundless love and mercy, He the ransom freely gave.

Sing, oh sing, of my Redeemer, with His blood, He purchased me.
On the cross, He sealed my pardon, paid the debt, and made me free.

VERSE 3

I will praise my dear Redeemer, his triumphant power I'll tell
How the victory he gives me over sin and death and hell.

Sing, oh sing, of my Redeemer, with His blood, He purchased me.
On the cross, He sealed my pardon, paid the debt, and made me free.

Sing, oh sing, of my Redeemer, with His blood, He purchased me.
On the cross, He sealed my pardon, paid the debt, and made me free.

9

·A TIME TO BUILD UP·

CONTEXT: *Nehemiah 4*

"WHEN YOU HEAR THE BLAST OF THE TRUMPET, RUSH TO WHEREVER IT IS SOUNDING. THEN OUR GOD WILL FIGHT FOR US!" NEHEMIAH 4:20

A PAIR OF Carolina wrens built a nest between two flowerpots on my deck. These small birds are industrious builders. I watched with delight as they manipulated twigs, pine needles, feathers, and blades of grass in their tiny, curved beaks. I couldn't tell mom from dad, but one of them was definitely in charge of decorating as I found several rejected items tossed from the worksite each day. Apparently, my contribution to the construction project was cleanup duty.

The finished home was both solid and cozy. The clever birds found a respectable moss supply. The entire nest was lined with a variety of green mosses. The grasses, twigs, and leaves were compacted tightly into a round shape with a tunnel-like entrance. The stronger, stiffer building materials were on the outside and the softer items, like the moss, the fluff of the dogs' undercoat, and feathers, were on the inside. It was truly a work to admire.

A few days after the nest was finished, I peeked inside. Mama Wren had deposited four tiny, brown-and-white-speckled eggs into her precious space. The incubation period for a wren is about two weeks. I try my best not to interrupt Mom while she sits on her clutch. Instead I wait with eager anticipation to meet her fuzzy-headed little brood.

I don't know much about construction, but I imagine that the bigger the project, the more challenging the process. With God's encouragement (divine intervention), the Israelites who returned to Jerusalem accomplished the task of rebuilding the temple. The temple was rebuilt (Zechariah), worship returned to the holy city (Ezra), and later, the walls and gates around Jerusalem were rebuilt (Nehemiah). So many stones replaced, so many hearts restored. God is in the construction business—He wants to build us up and He longs to bring us (back) to Him. He has done that in so many creative ways throughout history—and He does that for us today.

I think of Nehemiah's example. God inspired Nehemiah to rebuild the walls around Jerusalem. Nehemiah, in turn, inspired the families of Jerusalem in such a way that they completed the monumental project in an impossible fifty-two days. Nehemiah was an exceptional leader in many ways, but what I admire most was his ability to communicate with people in a way that reminded them of their purpose. Godly vision is a powerful motivator in the midst of a God-sized project.

The wrens chirp and chatter while I open my Bible to the book of Nehemiah. I settle on chapter 4, verses 6–21. Under Nehemiah's leadership, the people worked enthusiastically until about the halfway point in the project—when fatigue set in. Fatigue began feeding doubt. To make matters worse, enemies of the Jews threatened to kill the workers. The wall was only half-done, but the people were in danger of folding under the weight of fear and discouragement.

"Then the people of Judah began to complain, 'The workers are getting tired, and there is so much rubble to be moved. We will never be able to build the wall by ourselves.'" Nehemiah 4:10

I see the words. I feel the discouragement. I hear the whining! *Is that how I sound, Lord, when I am exhausted, angry, or undone?* When I am weak, the Enemy's claws scratch at my flesh looking for a way in. He knows my tender, vulnerable places.

The devil is on the prowl for any opportunity to minimize the work God wants to do in us and through us. The Enemy won't pass up an occasion to tear us down. We must not give him that opportunity! God's Word builds us up and prepares us for the schemes of the Enemy.

Proverbs tells us that "Where there is no vision, the people perish" (29:18 KJV). I memorized that translation years ago. The verse reminds me to keep my eyes on the assignment and my feet on the path forward. This translation also points to the great value of a God-given vision. Nehemiah understood the power of communicating a purpose and vision as a means of encouragement and motivation.

Nehemiah's vision was not simply to rebuild a structure. He was grieved by the condition of the city and the people. He desired to complete the wall in order to restore honor to God and hope to the nation of Israel. Nehemiah was prayerful at every step. God blessed Nehemiah's humble, available, reverent heart and pointed the way through every challenge. When the people were ready to give up, Nehemiah reminded them of their purpose and encouraged them to stay the course.

He told them, "'Don't be afraid of the enemy! Remember the Lord, who is great and glorious'" (Nehemiah 4:14). Nehemiah reminded them of God's faithfulness, refocused the people, and the work continued. With half the work left to go, he was an effective leader who was able to rally the people and complete the work.

Godly vision allows us to endure. How many more times during this season will the Spirit point me to this theme? He points me to "endurance." Is this the vision for every believer? Is this the vision that keeps us aligned with His good plan for us no matter our circumstances? Is this the vision that allows us to hear His praise, "well done, my good and faithful servant", to give us the ability to endure?

"DEAR BROTHERS AND SISTERS, WHEN TROUBLES OF ANY KIND COME YOUR WAY, CONSIDER IT AN OPPORTUNITY FOR GREAT JOY. FOR YOU KNOW THAT WHEN YOUR FAITH IS TESTED, YOUR ENDURANCE HAS A CHANCE TO GROW. SO LET IT GROW, FOR WHEN YOUR ENDURANCE IS FULLY DEVELOPED, YOU WILL BE PERFECT AND COMPLETE, NEEDING NOTHING."

JAMES 1:2-4

I think again of Nehemiah's story. He did nothing for his own glory. It was all for God. God's vision for God's glory. Nehemiah's heart was motivated by honoring God and building up the people of Israel. He inspired them to endure; he brought them the vision that mattered. God smiled on them all, I am sure!

Reflections

There is power in God's family encouraging one another. How can you encourage or serve someone else today?

Nehemiah changed the course of events when the people became discouraged. Let's consider his leadership style and how we can learn from him:

He is present. He oversees the project and is aware of everything that is happening.

He is perceptive. He listens and he responds to what the people are feeling.

He is proactive. He finds creative, timely solutions to the specific problems.

He is purposeful. He sees and shares the vision of a completed wall for God's glory.

He is positive. He is confident and focused on the goal—steadfast and immovable.

He is prayerful. Nehemiah's source of strength are his humble prayers.

How can you apply these "Nehemiah principles" in your life and current situations?

10

⚕ · REST IN THE STORMS · ⚕

CONTEXT: *Mark 4:35-41*

"WHEN JESUS WOKE UP, HE REBUKED THE
WIND AND SAID TO THE WAVES, 'SILENCE! BE
STILL!' SUDDENLY THE WIND STOPPED, AND
THERE WAS A GREAT CALM." MARK 4:39

SPA DAY AT the farm comes every six to eight weeks. The goats get their coats
brushed, their hooves trimmed, and an extra dose of vitamins and supplements. It's a
fun day for all of us and the goats enjoy the extra attention (and extra snacks!). I was
finishing the last goat when I heard the rumble of thunder in the distance. I picked up
the pace—but I wasn't fast enough.

A gale of wind ushered in dark clouds, a drop in temperature, and a roar of thunder.
Sheets of rain and lightning broke through the darkness and we all ran for the cover
of the small barn. The barn roof is metal and the torrent resonated on the roof like an
angry hare pounding on a kettle drum. Twelve goats, a very large Livestock Guardian
Dog, five chickens, and I sheltered in the thick hay under that noisy metal roof while
the rain pounded down. The roar of the thunder rivaled a freight train. Trees swayed
and the rain blew sideways.

I looked around at the goats as they calmly divided into their family groups. Moms
and daughters pawed at the hay and snuggled into sleeping piles. Sisters bent their

knees and settled into a comfortable place with a good view. Some of them took a nap. Some of them chewed their cud. Some of them watched the ducks, who splashed in the puddles outside the door. No one worried. No one was restless, anxious, or afraid. No one was trying to solve a problem or figure a way out. Every single animal rested quietly and waited for the storm to pass.

There wasn't anywhere to go. There wasn't anything to do. I settled in the hay next to Luna. I rested my head on her warm, silky belly. I waited with them. I felt the damp, cool air. I smelled the fresh, sweet hay. I listened to the goats chew (and snore). I watched the ducks play. Rain thrummed steadily on the roof. It was peaceful—in the storm.

I closed my eyes and let the rhythm of the rain slow my breathing. I let the warmth of Luna's belly and the sounds of contentment still my heart.

Is this how Jesus slept on the boat? Was He so completely at peace that the storm that raged around Him didn't wreck Him? It didn't even wake Him.

Turn with me to Mark 4:35–41.

The disciples were crossing the lake in a small boat. Very suddenly, a fierce storm arose. The winds and waves challenged the tiny vessel and the boat filled with water. The disciples were distressed, anxious, and afraid, yet Jesus slept. The disciples woke Jesus and seemed almost hysterical as they practically accused Him of not caring if they drowned.

We know that God cares deeply when His people are afraid or threatened. The disciples knew that too—but in a state of panic, they spoke boldly and wrongly. Jesus responded. He commanded the storm to cease—"Silence," "Be still."

It is extraordinary to me that Jesus calmed the storm with a simple statement the moment that the disciples brought Jesus into their fears. Jesus didn't hesitate; He did not scold or instruct. He took care of the storm first.

Bring Jesus into your storm and He will respond. Confess your fears to Him and invite the Spirit to guide you. Confess. Invite. Listen.

Jesus saved the reproof for second. When the water was still and the storm was gone, Jesus asked, "Why are you afraid?" He pointed to the relationship between fear and faith. "Do you still have no faith?" "Faith over Fear" looks good on a T-shirt or a coffee mug, but are we truly living that message?

When we are afraid or anxious, it is often because we forget that God is in control—or perhaps we have not forgotten but, instead, have not yielded control in the first place.

Notes

Look back at verse 35: "Jesus said to his disciples, 'Let's cross to the other side of the lake.'" Jesus gave instructions. He was going to preach on other side of the lake. The disciples doubted Jesus' ability to follow through with His plan when they allowed fear to send them into a panic. How many times have you done that? Doubt creeps in, worries expand to full-blown fear—and we change course. Remember that God is not the Fear Bringer; that's the Enemy talking. Where is your confidence placed: In God's plan? In yourself? In your circumstances?

As a believer, Jesus is *in* our boat! He abides in our heart. The Holy Spirit *lives in us*. When we trust that God is in control, we do not have to bow to the specter of fear. We can sleep through the storms with perfect peace because we know that God will get us to the other side.

"HE [GOD] WILL COVER YOU WITH HIS FEATHERS. HE WILL SHELTER YOU WITH HIS WINGS. HIS FAITHFUL PROMISES ARE YOUR ARMOR AND PROTECTION."

(PSALM 91:4)

Underline "His faithful promises." Circle "armor." God's promises are what protect us in all circumstances. We have to know His promises to feel secure with His plan.

Reflections

Have you fully surrendered your life to God, trusting that He is in control? If not, in what areas do you struggle to release control to God?

Jesus asked, "Why are you afraid?" Think about that and confess to Him: What are you afraid of?

What practices help you to trust that God is good and you are safe with Him?

11

❧ · UNREALIZED EXPECTATIONS · ❧

CONTEXT: *John 19:25-27*

"WHEN JESUS SAW HIS MOTHER STANDING THERE
BESIDE THE DISCIPLE HE LOVED, HE SAID TO HER,
'DEAR WOMAN, HERE IS YOUR SON.'" JOHN 19:26

SQUIRT IS ONE of our farm chickens. She is a black Rosecomb bantam hen. Rosecombs are heritage breeds and true bantams. She is a small, energetic, fancy girl with silky, iridescent feathers, white earlobes, and a precious red crown on top of her petite head. Squirt tips the scales at less than two pounds but possesses an enormous mama's heart. Our girl sat faithfully for three weeks on three perfectly formed eggs hoping to hatch a tiny brood. Day twenty-one passed and no eggs hatched.

Day twenty-two, and no peeps. I held a flashlight against the eggs. The light revealed a silhouette of what was inside the eggs. This is an age-old method that farmers call "candling." An open flame, or candle, was the source of light before flashlights were available, hence the reference to a candle. The light of my flashlight shone through Squirt's eggs. I saw only fluid, no outline of chicks.

These eggs were not fertilized. No amount of sitting on unfertilized eggs will produce chicks. Squirt squawked fiercely in protest when I removed her eggs. All of her determination, perfect planning, and faithful effort were not going to yield her heart's desire. I am sorry for Squirt. She did everything right. This was not her intended outcome.

I knew that the eggs were not viable, but I could not explain that to a very disappointed, broody chicken. God continues to use this farm and the rhythms of nature to teach me powerful spiritual lessons. This is one of those lessons.

Let's leave the chicken for a moment and walk through some human dilemmas—and then through the scriptures God gives as balm to our wounds.

How do we reconcile pain and faith when we wake to a broken dream or a crushed hope? How do we manage to step forward when we have lost something we barely had a chance to hold? How do we honor Christ *in* us while we struggle with disappointment, frustration, and/or grief?

I am getting more practice with this than I would like—but, with each loss, God steps in and provides one more glimmer of what heaven will be like. Through His Word, He opens a tiny crack in my soul for sheer joy to bleed through and bring comfort. Every. Time.

Let's take a moment to make it personal. What are some situations that have introduced you to loss, grief, or disappointment?

The job opportunity that was so perfect it was practically created for you—but went to someone else?

The highly anticipated, greatly celebrated, already loved child—who did not arrive?

An unthinkable diagnosis imposing unwelcome limits on your body or on your time?

A cherished relationship broken beyond any conceivable means of repair?

That hollow, empty place at the table, on the couch, in the bed—that irrepressible quiet of a life partner who left this world before you?

We worship a God who is personal. He has a personal response for every one of our losses. Scripture shows us what Jesus did for His own earthly mother. Turn to John 19:25–27 in your Bible, or read along with the NLT version provided below.

"STANDING NEAR THE CROSS WERE JESUS' MOTHER, AND HIS MOTHER'S SISTER, MARY (WIFE OF CLOPAS), AND MARY MAGDALENE. WHEN JESUS SAW HIS

MOTHER STANDING THERE BESIDE THE DISCIPLE HE LOVED, HE SAID TO HER, 'DEAR WOMAN, HERE IS YOUR SON.' AND HE SAID TO THIS DISCIPLE, 'HERE IS YOUR MOTHER.' AND FROM THEN ON THIS DISCIPLE TOOK HER INTO HIS HOME."

Are you a mother? I am already completely undone imagining the agony Mary must have felt as she witnessed the crucifixion of her own perfect, beloved son. Where were the disciples? All but John had scattered in fear. He was there with Mary. The mother of Jesus stayed as close to her dying son as the soldiers would allow. Even if Mary understood Jesus' redemptive plan, living through this horror cannot be a mother's dream.

Matthew (27:55) and Mark (15:40) record that the women watched from a distance. But it seems likely that the fearful disciples were *also* watching from a safe distance. John, the disciple who was there, recorded that they were "near the cross." They were standing together and close enough to hear the dying Christ's final words.

Matthew Henry, in his classic commentary, writes about this text: "We do not find his mother wringing her hands or making a final outcry; but standing by the cross, and her friends with her. Surely she and they were strengthened by a divine power to this degree of patience. We know not what we can bear till we are tried, and then we know who has said, My grace is sufficient for thee."[7]

I love that perspective. It refocuses me.

Whatever challenge, whatever disappointment, whatever loss you and I face today, we can remember that as Christ abides in us, we have the grace and strength we need to persevere. When we are overwhelmed, divine power is the desired destination. We can't do it alone—but we are never alone! Christ in us *is* the divine strength that moves us forward. He charts our course and sets our pace. It is when we yield to His Presence that we experience His plan.

In verse 26, Jesus "tenderly provides for his mother" (Matthew Henry p. 1621). In our culture, hearing a son address his mother as "dear woman" sounds stiff or unfeeling. That is not what this is. Jesus was sensitive to His mother's feelings. Instead of breaking her into tiny, shattered, emotional pieces by calling her "mom"—Jesus directed her to a new relationship as He passed her to His beloved friend and disciple John, who took Mary as his own mother in that moment.

---

7 Henry, Matthew: *Matthew Henry's Concise Commentary on the Whole Bible*. (Zondervan, 1961), 1621.

Pain serves a purpose. I have disciplined myself not to ask why in the midst of loss. Instead, I want to know *what*. What does God want me to see or understand? What does He want me to let go of or to pick up? Most of the time, I have to stop thinking about myself to see it. I need my eyes on Him. When I seek *His* face, He will reveal His heart!

Reflections

Let's look back to the list of painful situations. God's Word offers scriptures that lead us away from a downward spiral of sorrow and into His divine appointment. Here are some to meditate on:

The job: Matthew 6:26; Proverbs 3:5

The miscarriage: Lamentations 3:17–24; Psalm 34:18

The diagnosis: Isaiah 41:10; John 10:10

The broken relationship: Matthew 11:28; Philippians 4:6–7

Death of a loved one: Revelation 21:4; Psalm 147:3

Do you have a personally meaningful Scripture that you go to for comfort and focus?

Listen to "Even If" by Mercy Me as you color the next page and shift your focus.

12

A WARM BATH MAKES EVERYTHING BETTER

CONTEXT: *Luke 10:38-42*

"THERE IS ONLY ONE THING WORTH
BEING CONCERNED ABOUT. MARY HAS
DISCOVERED IT, AND IT WILL NOT BE
TAKEN AWAY FROM HER." LUKE 10:42

MY CHARMING six-year-old duck has a strong personality. Poppy is assertive. She is loud and feisty. She is smart and curious. She knows that I am her worm-hunting partner, treat-bringer, and fresh water keeper. She comes running when I enter the pasture. But Poppy hasn't been herself for a day or two.

I spend hours in the pasture every day. I know my animals as well as they know me. They can't speak to me with words, but they speak clearly with their behavior. Poppy is typically the duck leading the charge on forage patrols. She is the one who quacks the loudest and runs the fastest. Yesterday, she spent time alone under the chicken coop—then under the goat bench. "Alone" was my first hint that something was amiss. This is not normal behavior for Poppy.

I picked her up and she didn't argue. I did not see any obvious wound, break, or tear. I gently stroked her long, elegant neck and asked for a clue. *How do I help you, my girl?* She sat quietly on my lap for a good ten minutes before she asked to get down.

Some of Poppy's symptoms pointed me to the possibility that she was "egg bound." This happens when an egg does not pass through the oviduct and is essentially stuck. This is not uncommon, but it is life-threatening. An Internet search pointed me to a warm bath for Poppy. The warmth of the water helps the duck's abdomen to relax and can help move the egg along.

I set up our guest bathroom as a spa for my very special guest. I filled the tub with warm water and dimmed the lights. I had a soft towel ready for her after her soak. I made sure it was quiet and the cat couldn't get in. Then, I gathered Poppy in my arms and carried her to her soaking appointment.

I slowly lowered Poppy in the water, not sure what to expect. She appeared to be pleasantly surprised. She made no attempt to get out of the tub and settled into the warm water and wiggled her tail feathers. She dunked her head and tasted the bath water. I am positive that she liked it. She swam around the tub. She looked up, down, and all around the unfamiliar environment with curiosity but not fear. The spa seemed to be relaxing her as intended.

After a good, long soak, I wrapped Poppy in the extra-soft spa towel and carried her back outside. Within the hour, Poppy had passed an extra-large, soft-shelled egg.

Not all of my farm stories get to end like this one, but I am so thankful that Poppy is herself again. She honked her hello to me bright and early this morning—ready as ever for her day.

What about us? When we are "stuck," is God prompting us to rest? Paralyzed, uncertain, uncomfortable—are those the times not to work harder and push through, but instead lean into His comfort, guidance, and wisdom? There are times when it is okay, even life-giving, to do nothing but soak!

READ LUKE 10:38–42.

I have to admit that I never liked this story because I understood Martha's frustration. As a firstborn, ambitious "doer" and mom, I related to Martha. Goodness, someone had to prepare the meal, right? That person was almost always me, so I read these verses from Martha's perspective. Since I related to Martha, I took Jesus' response as a personal scolding for doing what seemed obviously necessary. Through the lens of a new believer, the whole scenario just seemed a little unfair.

I see it differently today, decades into my walk with the Lord. The Spirit moves me to the details—to the heart—because that was where Jesus focused. It's a different story when we consider the heart and attitudes rather than the personalities.

Verse 40 reveals that Martha was "distracted by the big dinner she was preparing." "Distracted" was translated from the original Greek word *periespato*.[8] It means to draw away, to be over-occupied, cumbered, troubled, distressed. Martha wasn't merely feeding the disciples, she was preparing the Pinterest-perfect dinner party. In her excitement to see and serve Jesus, she was going over the top.

Celebrating and honoring someone we love with a lavish meal is certainly not a sin—but this was not the right time for extravagance. Jesus' time on earth, time to spend with the people He loved the most, was getting shorter. This was a time for sharing bread and soup, and being together.

Jesus didn't want a dinner party. He wanted to share His gospel message. He wanted to teach and prepare His disciples. He wanted Martha to be part of that too. He wasn't "scolding" Martha (as I believed as a child). In his commentary, Matthew Henry says, "He (Jesus) speaks as one in earnest, and deeply concerned for her welfare. Those who are entangled in the affairs of this life are not easily disentangled."[9] Jesus is disturbed by the excessiveness of Martha's efforts that are preventing her from sitting (and soaking) in Jesus Himself, resting at His feet, and listening to His teaching.

There are times to sit and soak in His Word and to be in His Presence—and nothing else. Henry continues, "Serious godliness is a needful thing, it is the one thing needful. Nothing but this will go with us into another world." I cannot recall a time when people spent more time, money, and effort on preparing the "perfect" everything—from birthday parties to gender reveals to prom invitations. I am not saying it isn't fun to prepare special things for special occasions, but ask God to keep your heart focused on what matters most.

Take time to sit at His feet daily. Ask for His wisdom in stewarding your time and resources well. I hear the Spirit reminding me that my time is always limited. How am I using it? Do I need a good soak today? Do you?

---

8 James Strong, *The New Strong's Expanded Exhaustive Concordance of the Bible*, Red letter ed. (Nashville: Thomas Nelson, 2010), 4049.
9 Matthew Henry: *Matthew Henry's Concise Commentary on the Whole Bible*. (Zondervan, 1961), 1621.

Reflections

Are you a "Mary" or a "Martha" personality by nature?

How does this story change when you see it from a heart-posture perspective instead of a personality perspective?

What are some occasions when you get too busy to study and pray—or is busyness your lifestyle?

What can you do to shift your schedule and make time to sit at the feet of Jesus?

How do you think your life will change if you spend time in His Word every single day? What would that look like?

Summer

THE SEASON EVERY CHILD ANTICIPATES WITH AS MUCH
EXCITEMENT AS CHRISTMAS—THE SEASON OF FREEDOM FROM
SCHOOL ROUTINES AND TRIPS TO OCEANS, CAMPGROUNDS,
AND AMUSEMENT PARKS. IT IS THE TIME FOR GATHERING,
FOR FAMILY BARBECUES, ENJOYING STICKY-SWEET POPSICLES,
ROASTING MARSHMALLOWS, AND CATCHING LIGHTNING BUGS!

HEART OF THE MATTER

CONTEXT: *Jonah*

"GUARD YOUR HEART ABOVE ALL ELSE,
FOR IT DETERMINES THE COURSE OF
YOUR LIFE." PROVERBS 4:23

I WAS IN SOUTHERN Florida visiting my son and his family on the first day of summer this year. This was the first (and possibly last!) time I have been this close to the equator. I have never felt summer quite like this. My mid-Atlantic body was stunned by the oppressive heat and swampy humidity the moment I deplaned. My son swears that you adjust (eventually) and enjoys being outside playing golf year-round. However, without adequate time to assimilate to the tropical Florida climate, I simply melted.

I look forward to each season, I really do. And I love the way the sun warms my old bones. But this was just too sudden a change for me to adapt. I have learned that I do best when I have time to acclimate to change. I don't enjoy quick pivots and sudden course corrections. I like time to adjust my perspective and plan for what may come. I like "transition time."

I watched my three-year-old grandson struggle with transitions this week as well. We enjoyed activities together inside and outside. He especially loves being outside. This precious child had no interest in leaving the park or the beach just because the adults decided it was "time to go." A three-year-old is focused on what is present—what they can experience tangibly right in from of them. This is what makes sense to their little toddler brains. My grandson, walking along the beach, holding his daddy's hand, splashing in the warm water, had no interest in shifting to a different place or activity. A typical toddler temper tantrum ensues when the joy of the present is interrupted.

Transition time is preferable, but we don't always get that, do we? We can (and do), even as adults, fight sudden interruptions, quick changes, or unanticipated shifts. I don't know if it was the beach setting or the theme of stubborn resistance that brought Jonah's story to mind, but it is the book of Jonah that gets my attention this morning. You can read the four short chapters in one sitting—and I recommend that you do!

Jonah is one of the Old Testament stories that is often retold to children, and so, perhaps, overlooked by adults. The remarkableness of a man being swallowed completely whole by a fish grabs the attention and imagination of a child. But does the improbability of the story make it unappealing to study later in life? If we have bypassed this book as an adult, we have missed out on one of God's most loving messages.

I use my study Bible. A study Bible is such a help. I highly recommend one if you don't already have one. I review the history, the themes, and main message of the book before I start reading the Scriptures. I tend to read and interpret something that I am looking for rather than the message that God planted in the text if I don't approach the Scriptures with the broad context. As I reviewed, I was reminded that God used Jonah to speak not to His precious Israelites, but to their Assyrian neighbors. Assyria was a powerful and wicked enemy of Israel.

Jonah lacks any flowery introduction. He got right to the point. Read Jonah 1:1–3 in your Bible. I have pulled the highlights from the NLT in the next paragraph:

"The LORD gave this message to Jonah, '"Get up and go to the great city of Nineveh. Announce my judgment against it because I have seen how wicked its people are.' But Jonah got up and went in the opposite direction."

Jonah got the "get up and go" message—but he ran the opposite way. God said go right; Jonah went left. We know how these things usually turn out. But look just a little deeper with me. The message of disobedience is clear—but the problem is not Jonah's behavior; the root of the problem is his heart. It's important to get to the heart of the matter—every time.

Jonah knew that God is merciful and compassionate. Jonah expected God to save the people rather than destroy them (Jonah 4:2-3). God's desire to help the nation of Assyria was not consistent with Jonah's desire to see them punished. Assyria was an enemy. Jonah didn't want them forgiven or excused. He didn't want any part of their "second chances." Jonah was angry about the whole thing because God's mercy for his enemies was not the desire of Jonah's heart.

Perhaps now this long-ago story feels a little more "grown up," and a little more current. I see my own sinful heart holding on to grievances and hoping for justice. I see my resistance to mercy when I feel I have been wronged. I want the end to be different. I want what I want.

Our hearts' desires are reflected all around us. Even in the areas of summer entertainment: watching a popular movie, I am convicted by my feeling of pleasure in seeing the "bad guy" eaten by the mutated, cinematic dinosaur. God's perspective is so different from ours in so many ways. It feels like an endless list sometimes.

The story of Jonah is a story of God reaching beyond His precious, chosen Hebrew people and into the world. He wants to save the world—even our enemies. Maybe especially our enemies. The book of Jonah gives us a glimmer of the salvation and redemption God planned for us through His son, Jesus. There is no one beyond His reach. There is no one, in His eyes, not worth saving. That's a hard truth for those of us who are addicted to justice. But what a beautiful message of God's love and grace. What a merciful and amazing God!

Like the toddler who struggles with transitions, I struggle to shift my mind and align my heart with God's. Help me, Lord, to want to pray for my "enemies." Help me to see how much better the world will be when every knee bows and every tongue acknowledges You—mighty, holy, perfect God (see Romans 14:11). Thank You, Jesus, for saving me, for calling selfish, simple me into Your family under heaven. I am so grateful. Help me to see what You see and love who You love. I need Your help with that! I do love and honor You and I thank You for Jonah's story and example.

Reflections

Can you think of an "enemy"—someone for whom you can pray?

How does seeing your adversary through the eyes of a loving God change your perspective?

Have you ever felt like saying no to a command given by God? What happened?

Ask God for His help to grow your heart, strengthen your mind, and soften your spirit. Write out your prayer and don't forget to date it.

2

❧ · SHOES OF PEACE · ❧

CONTEXT: *Ephesians 6:10-20*

"A FINAL WORD: BE STRONG IN THE LORD
AND IN HIS MIGHTY POWER. PUT ON ALL OF
GOD'S ARMOR SO THAT YOU WILL BE ABLE
TO STAND FIRM AGAINST ALL STRATEGIES
OF THE DEVIL. . ." EPH 6:10-12

SUMMER MORNINGS IN western Maryland are still relatively cool—before the heat rises and collides with the humidity. The rooster proudly proclaims the breakfast hour at Shepherd's Gate Farm. Dew glistens on the tall grasses revealing the elegant work of master web-spinners eager to catch a meal. Barn swallows swoop and dive for insects to feed their hungry broods. The deer and her spotted fawns head for the green meadow behind the pasture.

Early mornings are pleasant and my goats are slow to get up and moving. They don't have to work or wander for their breakfast. I fill their hay feeders and food troughs at the same times each morning and evening. They greet me with yawns and stretches today. Luna and Eve lift their sleepy heads and slowly lumber up and out of their hay beds to say hello.

I take my time to feed everyone. I feed our "senior girls" separately from everyone else. I mix an extruded hay pellet (easier to chew and digest) with beet shreds (for extra

vitamins and fiber) into a bowl and call Luna into the tack room. I sit on a stool and hold the bowl for my sweet old girl. While she enjoys her special meal, several wiggly, pink noses and curious whiskers peek out from under a nearby shelf.

Soon the whiskers, noses, and tiny pink paws are venturing out to my stool. Goats are sloppy eaters. Seeds and pellets drop to the floor. The mice are eager to scoop up the discarded edibles. If you know me at all, you know that I don't mind a few mice. Unfortunately, this season, we have more than a few mice living in, around, and under the tack room.

The barn cats do a good job managing the mouse population in the barn and near the main house. However, Jethro, our fearless guardian, will not allow the cats into the pasture and near his goats, ducks, or chickens. Jethro has decided that the cats are predators and lives by his "no predators allowed" rule.

Jethro is good at many things. He is an intimidating protector, a proficient guardian, an attentive nurse, a champion digger, a handsome ball of fluff and stuff—but he is a terrible mouser. As a result, we have a mounting mouse problem. In the absence of cats, another stealthy predator has found its way to the food source.

It was just a matter of time. My husband and I both knew it would happen. Black snakes have made their way to the tack room. Although this is flip-flop weather, I wear boots during snake season.

I don't want to interrupt the snake from doing its job to maintain a healthy natural balance here, but I do not like them and I don't enjoy sharing space with them. I protect my feet and ankles by wearing my muck boots in the field and in the tack room. I know I am safe with my boots on. I can complete my chores and let the snake do his work because I have the armor I need to feel protected from a potential bite. Additionally, I don't take my eyes off of the slithering reptile. I know it can't hurt me, but I am cautious and alert.

God calls us to suit up with a different type of armor—for a different type of enemy. He warns us against the schemes and strategies of the original deceiver. I turn to Ephesians 6:10–20. The apostle Paul cautioned us to utilize every piece of armor God provides in order to resist the devil.

VERSE 11 STARTS,

"PUT ON ALL OF GOD'S ARMOR."

Circle "all." Not a piece or a part or a few bits—we need it all. Neglect nothing.

What is the full and complete armor of God? According to Ephesians chapter 6, it includes:

Belt of Truth (v. 14)

Body armor of God's Righteousness (v. 14)

Shoes of Peace (v. 15)

Shield of Faith (v. 16)

Helmet of Salvation (v. 17)

Sword of the Spirit, God's Word (v. 17)

Prayer (v. 18)

My "snake boots" situation compels me to stay longer with the "shoes of peace" this morning.

I write the whole verse from the NLT:

"FOR SHOES, PUT ON THE PEACE THAT COMES FROM THE GOOD NEWS SO THAT YOU WILL BE FULLY PREPARED."

My pen circles the word "peace." I draw a two-sided arrow from the word "peace" to "the Good News." The good news is detailed in 1 Corinthians 15:3–6. The message of the gift of salvation through the death and resurrection of Jesus Christ brings us peace. Nothing can compete with that kind of peace.

Why shoes, I wonder? I put a box around "shoes." Is this part of the command to "go" (to go and make disciples)? Traveling (in those times, mostly walking) required a solid pair of shoes. Living according to my faith is also a "walking" metaphor. We want to walk our talk, right? It seems appropriate then, that living according to and spreading the good news that brings peace are aptly represented by a pair of shoes.

"So that" gets a double underline. "You will be fully prepared" gets a highlight. The reason for putting on these shoes, for sharing the gospel message—the source of peace—is to prepare our hearts and minds for whatever comes our way. It is the confidence in this message that solidifies our peace and strengthens our resolve to represent and to share the good news.

My last thought goes to the vigilance with which we must live out our faith. We must be alert and committed to what we believe. I will not turn my back on the snake in the tack room. Neither will I turn my back to the deceptive strategies of the Enemy. I can stand firm and sure-footed in my shoes of peace, confident in the message that I believe.

Reflections

Make a list of the pieces of armor described in verses 14–18. Which pieces of your own armor are most solid and secure?

Do any pieces of your armor need attention—a possible weak area that gives the Enemy a target or a way in?

Can you think of any area in which you are currently vulnerable? How will your armor help you manage?

How does wearing the armor of God give you peace?

What does that peace feel like?

3

❧ · VULNERABILITY IS THE WAY IN · ❧

CONTEXT: *James 1:1–27*

"FOR YOU KNOW THAT WHEN YOUR FAITH IS
TESTED, YOUR ENDURANCE HAS A CHANCE
TO GROW. SO LET IT GROW, FOR WHEN
YOUR ENDURANCE IS FULLY DEVELOPED,
YOU WILL BE PERFECT AND COMPLETE,
NEEDING NOTHING." JAMES 1:3–4

SUMMER HEAT WAVES crash into Maryland in July and August. The heat is oppressive, even dangerous, for days at a time. As summer progresses, dirt and dust peek through faded grasses that have grown thin, dry, and prickly. The beautiful shades of spring green have disappeared. Garden plants look sad and desperately wilted—constantly begging for the hose.

Barn fans run from sunrise to sunset. The goats lie still and silent in the shade. Jethro naps in the soft, dirt bed this champion digger has made for himself. I replace water three times a day for the animals when it's hot like this.

The ducks are especially eager to see me at midday. Cool, refreshing water flows from the pump and their bills scoop it out as soon as it hits the buckets. They bob and splash in the kiddie pool with the exuberance of the preschoolers for which it was made. Quacking and honking with delight, the ducks dive into the clear, revitalizing waters—and I wish I could join them!

It is late afternoon and the air is still. There is barely a breeze. The distinctive screech of a hawk breaks though the calm like nails on a chalkboard. The hair stands up on the back of my neck at the sound.

There are two juvenile hawks in residence in our woods. They do not seem eager to leave. These young predators are noisy. It's almost as though they are practicing their fierce calls. They repeat a shrill, hoarse screech to proclaim their territory. I do not like having predators so close. Even a young hawk can kill or injure my ducks and chickens. I find myself counting my birds several times a day.

The hawks screech all day long and the repetition concerns me. These young hawks may just be practicing—but thinking about the story of the boy who cried wolf, I wonder if Jethro will learn to tune out the danger. I need Jethro to do what he does best and protect the ones who cannot defend themselves.

God points me to a spiritual lesson—a spiritual inventory.

What "predators" are in my space, in my home or community, or in my head? What schemes are growing so slowly around me that I don't even notice the threat? What is prowling around just outside my door that is not getting my attention?

The Scriptures teach me to "be alert," "be on guard," "be aware" of the schemes of the Enemy. God doesn't tell me to be afraid, but rather, "to stand firm" and "to be ready" (1 Peter 5:8; 1 Corinthians 16:13).

Lord, lift the veil that covers my eyes. Help me to see what is not yet obvious. Dear Jesus, break the boundaries that are slowly forming around my heart. Help me to stay soft and open to You and to the ones You love.

This has been a long and difficult season in several areas of my life. Some days the oppressive heat outside matches

the heaviness of my mood inside. There is pain that brings defensiveness and loss that I cannot control. Like Paul's "thorn," I see no relief in sight. I am reminded that God is not in a hurry and I need to be patient. I have also learned that anger breeds more anger. I don't want to live angry and wounded, so I lean into His Word daily. I can't endure this without Him.

He whispers. I listen.

Is it possible that vulnerability is the way to stay safe in His arms? Even better, is it the path to holy transformation?

Predators are strong, fierce, and intimidating. Matching strength to strength, threat to threat, and armor to armor is the world's way. God does not work the way the world does. When Jesus entered Jerusalem in the final days of His earthly life, His followers were looking for a leader and king—one powerful enough to conquer their Roman oppressors. Jesus answered the threats against Him by submitting to death on a cross. Absolute power was absolute vulnerability. God's way is not the world's way.

I walk cautiously to the door of vulnerability and I knock.

As believers, "We now have this light shining in our hearts, but we ourselves are like fragile clay jars containing this great treasure" (2 Corinthians 4:7). Scripture points to how fragile we are. It is the power of God in us, His purposeful work in and through us, that gives us our value and our strength.

Recognizing my vulnerability, my weakness, and my inability gives God room to work. I am malleable when I am vulnerable. He can transform even this stony heart into a heart of flesh (Ezekiel 36:26) when it is submitted to His hand. God's power, His strength, His wisdom—His GRACE—can only live in a surrendered heart.

Gently, He reminds me again of His paradoxes: softness invites strength, tenderness grows courage, and yielding brings power. I hear, Give it to Me, my girl. Give it to Me. He does the work when we let Him.

I revisit God's armor (Ephesians 6): truth, peace, faith, salvation, God's Word and His righteousness, and prayer. Not one of those items is fierce by our world's definition, yet they are all we need to stand firm, confident, and courageous. We can face any enemy, endure any pain, and bear any disappointment when the power of His grace is secure in our hearts.

He is Emmanuel. He is with us through it all. He brings blessings in the waiting. He brings joy in course corrections and peace in unexpected beginnings. He gives me all I need.

Time in His Presence refreshes my soul and encourages my heart. Thank You for leading me, Lord.

I finish my farm chores as strong winds usher in cool air. I stretch my arms wide like a cruising barn swallow and allow the winds to flow over me. The cool air brings instant relief to my hot skin. I smell the rain. The storm is close. Perhaps, on a different day, I would run for cover—but today, after completing farm chores in sweltering heat, I embrace the blessing of cool wind and the rain on the horizon. I walk slowly to the house inviting the swirls of blissfully chilled air to envelope me while I wait for the parched ground to receive the soaking. And I am not afraid.

Reflections

It isn't easy to be vulnerable. Most of us protect our hearts and egos from other people because we don't want to be rejected or hurt. Being vulnerable with God is not the same as being vulnerable with a person. How is it different?

We know that olives must be pressed to produce the oil we desire; gold and silver must be melted to form a new shape; diamonds are formed by intense heat and pressure. The Spirit of God transforms a believer over time, experience, and often by pain. How can you shift your perspective away from pain and pity and to the process God is pursuing (our hearts' transformation)?

The process of transformation happens over our lifetime, a life of walking with God. This process is called sanctification. Can you think of and praise God for some of the changes He has already made in your heart and mind?

Perhaps you are in a trouble-free season in your life. What can you do to strengthen your faith and prepare for a season of challenge?

Listen to "Lord of Hosts" as you contemplate God in your challenges and color the next page.

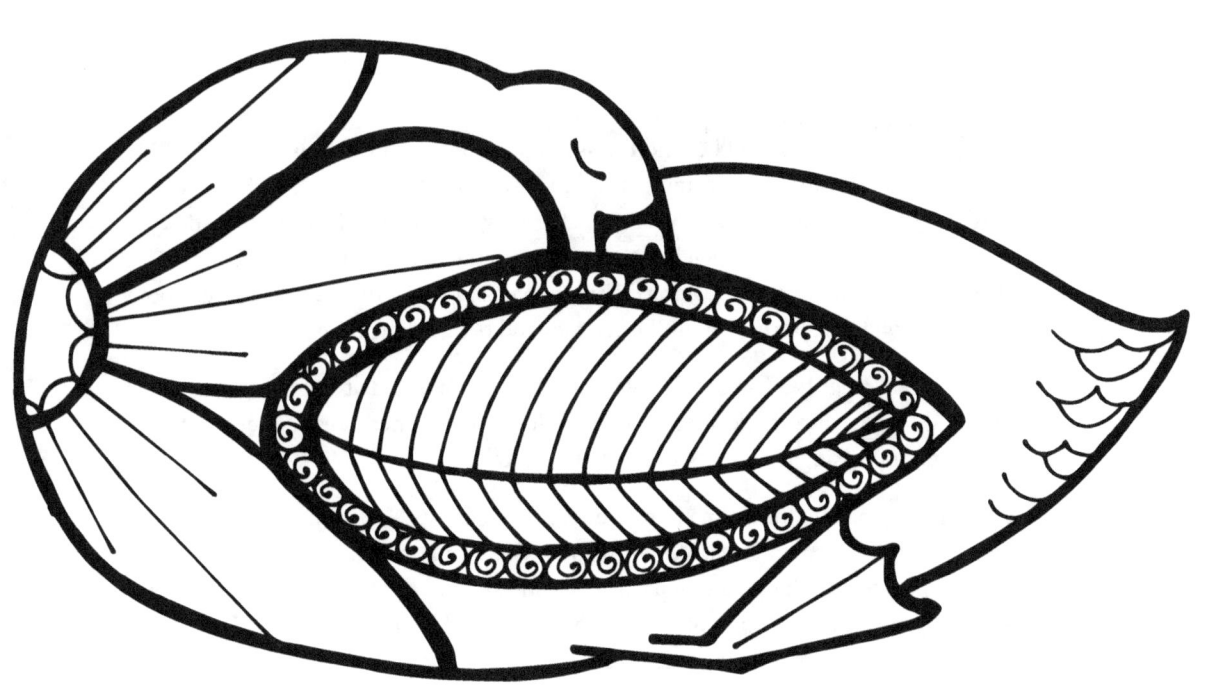

4

❧ · ASK, SEEK, AND KNOCK · ❧

CONTEXT: *Matthew 7:7-11*

"KEEP ON ASKING, AND YOU WILL RECEIVE
WHAT YOU ASK FOR. KEEP ON SEEKING, AND
YOU WILL FIND. KEEP ON KNOCKING, AND THE
DOOR WILL BE OPENED TO YOU." MATTHEW 7:7

IT'S EARLY MORNING and the sky is blue, but the air is heavy and thick. My boots crunch through the drying grass on my way to the pasture. The hard August earth is unyielding under my boots. I reach for the gate. The metal hardware is still cool this early in the day but the latch is tight. I push, pull, and wrestle with the fastening. It requires two hands this morning. I set my load of hay on the ground and use both hands to wiggle the latch-arm until it releases and the gate swings open.

Summer brings heat, and in my beautiful state of Maryland, it also brings humidity. Humidity makes heat stick. It's like an extra layer of summer, pressing fever into my pores and increasing the sweat quotient a few notches.

Humidity affects things made of wood, like gateposts. Wooden posts absorb the moisture in the air and swell. When metal latches are attached to wooden gateposts (like mine), the swelling causes problems with alignment. As the wood swells and shifts, the latch-arm does not fit easily into the strike plate. Every summer day, I tussle with the gate to get in and out of the pasture. It is a temporary but annoying problem.

This morning, I move along with the troublesome gate in my mind. God's Spirit hovers and I linger. I love gate/door analogies. Today I think of the extra effort it takes to get into the pasture and care for the animals. I can't quit just because it's difficult or annoying. Persistence brings life.

"Ask, seek, knock" comes to mind from Matthew chapter 7. How badly do I want to know Him, to know what He has to say? How much effort will I apply to go further, dig deeper, and understand more?

Ask in prayer. I must use my words.

Seek in Scripture. I must use my mind.

Knock in action. I must use my life.

His Spirit, His *Ruah* (Hebrew for "breath") initiates this love relationship. I respond. The harder I lean into Him, the more He reveals to me. The longer I live, the less interested I am in living for myself. He shows me a new way to live. I wiggle the gate daily—I want to get in.

After chores, I settle in with my Bible at the kitchen island. Dogs snore softly at my feet while I turn the precious tissue pages to Matthew 7:7–8.

"ASK, AND IT WILL BE GIVEN TO YOU; SEEK, AND YOU WILL FIND; KNOCK, AND IT WILL BE OPENED TO YOU. FOR EVERYONE WHO ASKS RECEIVES, AND THE ONE WHO SEEKS FINDS, AND TO THE ONE WHO KNOCKS IT WILL BE OPENED." (ESV)

I circle "Ask" in my Bible. "Ask" in this context means to request or petition through prayer. Prayer is a holy conversation. It is time and attention shared with my loving, trustworthy heavenly Father. It is pouring out my heart, knowing that I am heard, loved, and adored. It is sweet time with Jesus in the give-and-take (speaking and listening) of blessed communion.

The more time I spend with Him in prayer, the more He directs my heart and requests. I want my requests to be aligned with His will and His purpose. With eternity in mind, my petitions are different than if all I am thinking about is my present happiness. I believe He wants us all to grow beyond simple, selfish designs.

I ask to see what He sees and to be alert to opportunities to serve that He puts in my path. I often struggle with gentleness, so I ask for strength of meekness and pure loving-kindness that honors Him in my interactions with others. What do I need today that I don't see? He will show me while I wait.

I circle "seek." "Seek" in this verse feels like more than casual looking. It seems to me to be a more ambitious searching and effortful endeavor. I immediately think of several Bible verses that use the word "seek":

"YOU WILL SEEK ME AND FIND ME WHEN YOU SEEK ME WITH ALL YOUR HEART."

JEREMIAH 29:13 NIV

"THOSE WHO SEEK ME DILIGENTLY WILL FIND ME."

PROVERBS 8:17 ESV

"BUT SEEK FIRST THE KINGDOM OF GOD AND HIS RIGHTEOUSNESS, AND ALL THESE THINGS WILL BE ADDED TO YOU."

MATTHEW 6:33 ESV

"SEEK THE LORD AND HIS STRENGTH; SEEK HIS PRESENCE CONTINUALLY!"

1 CHRONICLES 16:11 ESV

"WITH MY WHOLE HEART I SEEK YOU."

PSALM 119:10 ESV

"THE LORD IS GOOD TO THOSE WHO WAIT FOR HIM, TO THE SOUL WHO SEEKS HIM."

LAMENTATIONS 3:25 ESV

"FOR THUS SAYS THE LORD TO THE HOUSE OF ISRAEL: 'SEEK ME AND LIVE.'"

AMOS 5:4 ESV

"YOU HAVE SAID, 'SEEK MY FACE.' MY HEART SAYS TO YOU, 'YOUR FACE, LORD, DO I SEEK.'"

PSALM 27:8 ESV

Jesus, thank You for showing me that my focus needs to be on You, not on my challenges. You show me what I need to see when I seek Your face. Thank You for shifting my attention. Thank You for the illumination of truth that comes with basking in the glory of Your light over the distractions I encounter in the shadows. Keep me here, dear Lord, right here in Your Presence, in Your sweet and perfect peace.

I circle "knock." This is my effort, my response to His Spirit, the prompts and whispers. I remain alert, present, available, obedient, and persistent. This is where I wiggle the gate. Even when it sticks, I want to get in. I want to be ever closer to God. I am desperate to be close to Him. I won't give in or give up in the face of difficulty. Lord, I lean on You; I lean in hard. I want more and more of You!

I close my Bible and I close my eyes. I think of the gate again. How desperate am I to get in? With all my heart, I

want to pass through the narrow gate that is the Shepherd's Way. Lord, I ask You to give me courage and opportunity, through my choices, my words, and my life, to share the way through that beautiful gate. I seek Your will and purpose for all of my moments, trusting You as I step, leap, or stumble forward. I knock persistently until glory comes and I am finished here.

Reflections

"My heart has heard you say, 'Come and talk with me.'" And my heart responds, 'Lord, I am coming.'" Psalm 27:8

Do you find yourself desperate to spend time with the Lord in this season of life? How does spiritual desperation feel to you—what words describe a heart that yearns for more of Him?

What are you desperate for today?

Do you need a fresh perspective? Ask God to give it to you. He will!

Write out your prayer here. Don't forget to date it.

5

℘ · IT'S OUR TURN · ℘

CONTEXT: *Ruth*

"THEN NAOMI SAID TO HER, 'JUST BE PATIENT,
MY DAUGHTER, UNTIL WE HEAR WHAT
HAPPENS. THE MAN WON'T REST UNTIL HE
HAS SETTLED THINGS TODAY.'" RUTH 3:18

IT IS A GORGEOUS summer evening—the kind of evening you hope for when you've planned an important outdoor social event. It's a cozy 80 degrees. The low humidity and gentle breeze make it feel cooler. The sky is clear and blue, washed clean by last night's storm. I do not have a social event planned. My husband isn't even home. I am sitting on the back steps of my house by myself, watching my goats in the field and enjoying every sweet moment of this perfect stillness.

Luna initiated the pasture parade this evening. When one goat leaves the barn to browse in the pasture, the rest fall in line behind the leader. Luna started slowly up the field for a snack. One by one, I watched Maddie, Molly, Mai Tai, Fern, Eleanor, and then Eve join the meandering walk-and-munch procession. Step, nibble, step, step, nibble.

The "babies" (these full-grown four-year-olds are the youngest of the herd and so they forever retain the designation "babies") were busy playing when the rest of the herd moved out, rising on hind legs then falling to butt heads, wagging tails, jumping, and pushing the way goats play—Allie, Grace, Lacey, and Meg scampered to catch up when they suddenly realized they were the only ones left in the barn.

I laughed as the babies caught up quickly and immediately settled into a browsing pace. I smiled at Luna for leading the way. She does not do that often anymore. In fact, there are more and more days that she rests her stiff joints in the barn while the herd wanders out. It makes me happy to see her lead now and then.

My sweet old girl reminds me of the brevity of life and the value of appreciating each season, every moment, all our experiences and opportunities. There is so much that I understand and appreciate now that wasn't even on my radar in my twenties or thirties. What a difference a life lived makes in our appreciation of everything. Everything!

The book of Ruth is one of my favorite stories—for so many reasons. In my previous studies, I have concentrated my attention on Ruth (and Boaz, her redeemer). The book is named for Ruth, but authorship is traditionally awarded to the prophet Samuel. Samuel tells the story from Ruth's mother-in-law, Naomi's, point of view. With my senior girl, Luna, in mind, I am looking closer at Naomi today.

The Bible story is about redemption and God's faithfulness to provide for us. Ruth is a short story told in just four chapters. Things don't start well for Naomi. Naomi, her husband, and their two sons left Israel due to a famine. They moved to Moab, a country often in conflict with Israel. Her husband died and her sons married Moabite (not Hebrew) women. By the end of chapter one, poor Naomi is as miserable as Job. She lost her home, her country, her family, and her financial support.

Naomi was shattered by her grief. "Don't call me Naomi…Instead call me Mara, for the Almighty has made life very bitter for me" (Ruth 1:20). She expressed her brokenness with honesty, didn't she? Even if it sounds like a pity party on paper, I believe that God honors our authentic communication. He knew her heart was broken. He would not leave her wrecked and alone.

We don't get to fast-forward through the unpleasant experiences. We have already agreed that the longer we live on this earth, the more encounters we will have with loss and pain. How do we, as followers of Jesus, deal with loss? Naomi's story tells me that it is appropriate to voice our feelings to God. I imagine that not only is this conversation with God admissible, it is necessary if we want to heal, to grow, to move forward—and to nurture our relationship with our Creator, the Lover of our soul. As Naomi poured her heart out to God, He heard her, and His plan to redeem her was already in place.

When I cry over my situation, my disappointment or regret, I imagine my heavenly Father lifting my chin, meeting my eyes, reminding me how much He cares. I don't have to wallow. I can grieve until I am ready to step forward trusting His plan and

purpose for every part of my life. He is standing by, ready to redeem a soft, obedient heart.

His holy assignments are not reserved for young, eager, beautiful, brilliant people. As long as our hearts are willing and our spirits are aligned with His, we are never past "useful" to our God. If Naomi had decided her turn was over, that it was time for the younger generation to take their turn, Ruth would not have won Boaz's attention. Naomi still had work to do.

Naomi carefully mentored her daughter-in-law. In doing so, she not only assured their physical survival but their spiritual legacy. The tone of this short story changes. Naomi sees a way out of their situation—perhaps she sees God's hand, His providence, as Ruth goes to work in the fields of a relative.

In the end, Boaz redeemed the family and married Ruth. They had a son. "Naomi took the baby and cuddled him to her own breast. And she cared for him as if he were her own" (Ruth 4:16). Naomi's heart was renewed, her life restored.

God wove a beautiful love story for Ruth and Boaz. Naomi played a significant role in the story—one that revealed not only God's intimate love and purpose for each one of us but also His greater plan for our salvation. Ruth's baby, the son that Naomi cuddled and loved, was Obed. Obed was the father of Jesse and grandfather of David, in the family line of Jesus—the Messiah, our perfect Redeemer.

Wow. The legacy of obedience, the faithfulness of God—a God who is in every detail—who does not let us sit brokenhearted and alone—writes my story too. We are never too old to play a role in the story God writes. We don't outgrow our "turn"—no matter the season, it is our turn.

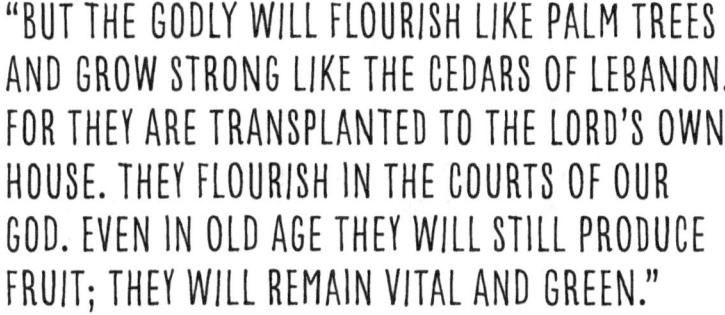

Reflections

Read these verses then reflect on the thoughts and questions on the next page.

"I WILL BE YOUR GOD THROUGHOUT YOUR LIFETIME—UNTIL YOUR HAIR IS WHITE WITH AGE. I MADE YOU, AND I WILL CARE FOR YOU. I WILL CARRY YOU ALONG AND SAVE YOU."

ISAIAH 46:4

"BUT THE GODLY WILL FLOURISH LIKE PALM TREES AND GROW STRONG LIKE THE CEDARS OF LEBANON. FOR THEY ARE TRANSPLANTED TO THE LORD'S OWN HOUSE. THEY FLOURISH IN THE COURTS OF OUR GOD. EVEN IN OLD AGE THEY WILL STILL PRODUCE FRUIT; THEY WILL REMAIN VITAL AND GREEN."

PSALM 92:12-14

"AND I AM CERTAIN THAT GOD, WHO BEGAN THE GOOD WORK WITHIN YOU, WILL CONTINUE HIS WORK UNTIL IT IS FINALLY FINISHED ON THE DAY WHEN CHRIST JESUS RETURNS."

PHILIPPIANS 1:6

What is something that you understand and can do now that you were unable to five or ten years ago?

Name something that you are pursuing over time to earn or accomplish (a long-term goal).

How has God provided course corrections for you along the way?

Have you given up on anything because of your age or season of life (too old, too young, too something else)? How does Naomi's story encourage you not to give up?

How has God equipped you to serve someone else?

6

❧ · AND YET... · ❧

CONTEXT: *Habakkuk*

"YET I WILL REJOICE IN THE LORD! I
WILL BE JOYFUL IN THE GOD OF MY
SALVATION!" HABAKKUK 3:18

INSECTS THRIVE IN the summer. Every crawling, flying, buzzing, six-legged creature seems to multiply in the heat. There are a few (butterflies, ladybugs, fireflies, and honey bees) that bring pleasure—but zillions more are pests. Insects are among those things I generally have to "put up with" at the farm.

One bright spot was discovering a variety of bugs one summer with my curious five-year-old granddaughter. We wore out our insect guidebook identifying the different species of colorful, crawly bugs. We designed a few different bug houses to hold them for observation (and playing). A jar with holes poked in the lid for the fireflies caught at dusk. A bug bucket for carrying our wiggly friends. A screened box for watching caterpillars make cocoons. My granddaughter's excitement with the tiny critters made some insects more interesting and even fun.

There are other insects, however, that are never going to make my "fun list." Flies, gnats, and wasps are at the top of the pest list. The farm introduced me to a wide variety of wasps. We have potter wasps, mud dauber wasps, paper wasps, and yellow jackets. I don't like any of those and am careful to steer clear of their nests. However, I am aware that even wasps were created for a purpose. Wasps keep our ecosystem balanced by controlling the caterpillar, fly, and spider populations.

The plethora of bugs at the farm reminds me of how important balance is to everything. As much as I dislike a swarm of gnats or the sting of a wasp, I remember that even those tiny, annoying insects have a significant purpose. As long as the earth is relatively healthy, insects will be part of our summers. Some things won't change, so, instead, we change our perspective.

The book of Habakkuk contains three chapters. It records a dialogue between the prophet Habakkuk and God. It was written during a time when evil kings reigned in Jerusalem and God's people were facing invasion and destruction. Not a happy time. And yet this tiny book has great purpose.

Habakkuk is used as a model for journaling our prayers. Habakkuk was unhappy and confused. He cried,

"WHY MUST I WATCH ALL THIS MISERY? WHEREVER I LOOK, I SEE DESTRUCTION AND VIOLENCE. I AM SURROUNDED BY PEOPLE WHO LOVE TO ARGUE AND FIGHT."

HABAKKUK 1:3

He wrote out his feelings and frustrations and he recorded the Lord's responses. The model is an excellent one for us to follow. I like to write my prayers in black ink. I write what I perceive to be responses from God's Spirit in a different color (purple or pink ink). I write out scriptures in still other colors. My pages are color-coded prayers, requests, and praises.

In addition to journaling methods, Habakkuk reminds us of the significance of waiting on the Lord.

"I WILL CLIMB UP TO MY WATCHTOWER AND STAND AT MY GUARD POST. THERE I WILL WAIT TO SEE WHAT THE LORD SAYS AND HOW HE WILL ANSWER MY COMPLAINT."

HABAKKUK 2:1

Habakkuk waited alone. He watched while he waited. He expected a response and was willing to be quiet while God worked. I love this reminder. How can I expect God to respond to my prayer if I do not wait patiently, faithfully, and expectantly for His response? I have the sense that Habakkuk was a little stubborn here. "I will wait right here until you answer me" kind of stubborn. I think I need more of that.

Habakkuk records God's response in chapter 2. I don't think it was the response Habakkuk was hoping for. God provided beautiful wisdom and prophecy, but He did not promise to deal with Habakkuk's current dilemma. And yet...

And yet, Habakkuk's perspective shifted. Chapter 3 is a completely different message and tone. Rather than crying, complaining, and worrying, Habakkuk's prayerful response was to sing praises to God.

"EVEN THOUGH THE FIG TREES HAVE NO BLOSSOMS, AND THERE ARE NO GRAPES ON THE VINES; EVEN THOUGH THE OLIVE CROP FAILS AND THE FIELDS LIE EMPTY AND BARREN; EVEN THOUGH THE FLOCKS DIE IN THE FIELDS, AND THE CATTLE BARNS ARE EMPTY, YET I WILL REJOICE IN THE LORD! I WILL BE JOYFUL IN THE GOD OF MY SALVATION!"

HABAKKUK 3:17–18

Wait. What?

Let me try that:

Even though my heart is breaking, I will trust You, Lord.

Even though I don't understand why this is happening, I will love You, Jesus.

Even though my diagnosis is scary, I will praise You, God.

Now you try it:

Even though (fill in your grief)

_____,

I will trust You, Lord.

Even though (fill in your disappointment)

_____,

I will love You, Jesus.

Even though (fill in your insecurity)

_____,

I will praise You, God.

Habakkuk's situation did not change. His heart and attitude did. He focused on God's authority, His sovereignty, and His faithfulness. Habakkuk could rest in God's perfect plan and in His perfect timing. God granted peace to Habakkuk because Habakkuk trusted God's goodness. He will do that for us too. I am so thankful that Habakkuk wrote out his prayers to guide us and encourage us.

I am thankful for his authenticity, for sharing his vulnerable heart. I am grateful for a prayer journal model I can follow in my conversations with my Father in heaven. I will praise Him with all my heart, even in the "and yet" seasons—because I know He is there and I know how much He cares. I trust His goodness always.

We can be sure that one day "the earth will be filled with an awareness of the glory of the LORD." (Habakkuk 2:14)

Reflections

Do you wait with expectation on the Lord? Why or why not?

Do you keep a prayer journal and a record of God's answers to your prayers? Does Habakkuk inspire you to do so?

God answers our prayers. "Yes," "no," and "wait" are all answers. Has he said no to your prayer requests? How do those answers look in hindsight?

Don't take my word for it. Take a few minutes to read these chapters yourself. Meditate on the verses. What is God's Spirit illuminating for you through Habakkuk's life?

Spend time in the following exercise: Play or read the old hymn, "It is Well with My Soul." Can you sing/say these words with spiritual conviction?

Look up Romans 8:28. How does that scripture verse apply to this message?

7

⊱· SUMMER MORNING TREASURE ·⊰

CONTEXT: *Psalm 150*

"LET EVERYTHING THAT BREATHES SING PRAISES THE LORD! PRAISE THE LORD!" PSALM 150:6

——————

I SO APPRECIATE the gentleness of summer mornings. Unhurried, peaceful stillness wrap around me like ever-loving arms. Summer sunrises over the pasture are my favorite. Warm, bright rays emerge from a cloudless sky spreading over the tender earth in a spirit of temperate awakening. Gentle. Sweet.

There are no extra steps to take in donning layers of clothing—stiff, quilted canvas coats or insulated boots. There is no bracing my face and body for the sting of bitter cold. There is no restriction of movement created by heavy outer layers and body posturing to avoid icy winds. I treasure the simplicity of summer mornings, of stepping into sunshine and comfortable temperatures. I take my time and cherish each morning, grateful for every precious, pleasant moment—knowing that the season is brief.

Luna loves her slow mornings too. My oldest doe, my snuggliest bug! My goats are the size of Labradors—and just as eager for petting and treats. Luna is usually the last to get up out of her hay bed but still the first to nuzzle in next to me. Those amber eyes search mine every morning. She walks with a limp these days but never misses a morning caress. Her "good morning" cuddles fill my entire being with joy.

This morning we sit together and watch the sun move higher in the sky. My arm wrapped around her soft, black neck, we chat about our plans for the day. Maddie and Molly join us—jockeying for a better position and potential chest rub. The girls lift their chins to the warming sun and close their eyes. It's going to be a good day.

Every day is a good day to "praise God from whom all blessings flow," but this morning, I can't stop myself even if I wanted to. It is moments like these when I am sure that even the rocks cry out in praise to Him (Luke 19:40).

My fingers twirl Luna's silky fur as the beams of the sun reach my cheeks. I soak in His glorious Presence while I praise Him for all He has done.

How many ways can we praise Him?

Mary praised with humble obedience.

Abraham and Sarah praised with family.

Joseph praised with reconciliation.

Moses praised with the law.

Miriam praised with joy and dancing.

Joshua and Caleb praised with courage.

Hannah praised with prayers.

Samuel praised with service.

David praised with songs and poetry.

Jonathan praised with friendship.

Solomon praised with wisdom.

Jeremiah praised with tears.

Ezra praised with worship.

Nehemiah praised with leadership.

Zechariah praised with small beginnings.

Matthew praised with His people.

Mark praised with strangers.

John praised with love.

Paul praised with letters.

Peter praised with holy boldness.

And I praise You with my words. My humble reflections of who You are to me: a mighty, loving, ever-present Father-Teacher-Counselor-Healer. Thank You, Lord, for every gift and challenge—for walking with me through it all. I thank You for another morning, for a blue sky and healthy animals. I thank You for a loving husband and gracious friends. Thank You for a healthy church body, a place to give and to grow. I thank You for another day to love and help others. Help me love them the way You do. Fill me with Your mercy and grace so that I may give it out in good measure. Thank You for Your Spirit that draws me near. I celebrate You. I honor and worship You. I am simply in awe of You and this life You've given me. I adore You and thank You, dear Jesus.

Psalm 150

Praise the LORD!

Praise God in his sanctuary; praise him in his mighty heaven!

Praise him for his mighty works; praise his unequaled greatness!

Praise him with a blast of the ram's horn; praise him with the lyre and harp!

Praise him with the tambourine and dancing; praise him with strings and flutes!

Praise him with a clash of cymbals; praise him with loud clanging cymbals.

Let everything that breathes sing praises to the LORD!

Praise the LORD!

Reflections

How can you praise Him today?

Do you have the habit of praising Him for His work in and around you?

How can you be more alert to the presence of God in your day to day activities?

My friend Lori has a wonderful routine of starting each day with gratitude. She names five things she is thankful for every day. Can you list five things that you are grateful for every day for five days?

8

FOLLOW WHERE THE SPIRIT LEADS

CONTEXT: *Isaiah 40:12-31*

"HE GIVES POWER TO THE WEAK AND STRENGTH
TO THE POWERLESS." ISAIAH 40:29

IT IS A WARM and humid afternoon in late August. The calendar says everything pumpkin spice is just around the corner, but the air is still heavy with summer. I walk out to the pasture to refresh the water buckets, check hay levels, and visit with my crew.

I am sweating and swatting at flies before I even get to the gate. Flies are unavoidable at the farm. We do as much as we can to minimize them but they are persistent pests. Today, the gnats are even peskier than the flies. Those tiny flying insects go right for the eyes. I tuck my chin and keep my head down to deter them. Still, they fly into my eyes and buzz around my ears in spite of all my hand flapping and chin tucking! Instead of a leisurely afternoon with the animals, I hurry through my chores so I can escape the bugs.

I have a "gnat hat" for days like this. It's really more of a mesh bag than a hat. I don a baseball cap and put the mesh bag over my head. The mesh lets me see and breathe, but the gnats can't penetrate the fabric barrier. The baseball cap keeps the mesh at a more comfortable distance from my face. It is useful but not at all fashionable. Not everything at the farm is beautiful.

It isn't lost on me that two of the ten plagues God sent to Egypt were gnats and flies. I don't want to minimize the plague-level apocalypse of annoying insects, but what was God thinking in sending those pests? I want to think more about that—in my cozy, bug-free, air-conditioned house!

"Seek me and you will find me...draw near to me and I will draw near to you" resonates in my mind as I take my Bible off the shelf. Can I find God's purpose even in gnats tangled in my eyelashes?

I open my Bible to Exodus. The plagues are described in chapters 7 through 11. After a review of the scriptures, I realize that a deep study might give me a clue about why God chose flies and gnats as plagues, but I will save that exhaustive study for another day. However, my review did remind me of something significant that I want to share here.

At one time, I thought that God sent the ten plagues like ten chances for Pharaoh to choose well and to release the Hebrews from slavery. But this story is not about a patient God who gives us many opportunities to choose to do the right thing (that might be true, but that is not this story).

God sent ten plagues not to change the heart and mind of an evil man and oppressive leader (Pharaoh), but, rather, to demonstrate the fullness of His power and justice to His beloved people.

God saved His people physically when He led them out of slavery in Egypt and into the promised land. He saves us spiritually by delivering us from the emptiness and evil of this world and into eternity with His own family.

The power and strength and justice of God deserves to be revered, respected, and held in awe. If we don't understand that sin—our sin—deserves the judgment of death, then we can't stand in awe of a God who saves us from that penalty. I soak in His sweet, loving Presence because He saved me from my own self and from a life of meaningless pursuits.

Instead of analyzing flies and gnats, I choose to focus on His power to save my repentant heart:

"O SOVEREIGN LORD! YOU MADE THE HEAVENS AND EARTH BY YOUR STRONG HAND AND POWERFUL ARM.

NOTHING IS TOO HARD FOR YOU! ...YOU ARE THE GREAT
AND POWERFUL GOD, THE LORD OF HEAVEN'S ARMIES."

JEREMIAH 32:17-18

"HAVE YOU NEVER HEARD? HAVE YOU NEVER
UNDERSTOOD? THE LORD IS THE EVERLASTING GOD,
THE CREATOR OF ALL THE EARTH. HE NEVER GROWS
WEAK OR WEARY. NO ONE CAN MEASURE THE DEPTHS
OF HIS UNDERSTANDING. HE GIVES POWER TO THE
WEAK AND STRENGTH TO THE POWERLESS."

ISAIAH 40:28-29

"JESUS LOOKED AT THEM INTENTLY AND SAID,
'HUMANLY SPEAKING, IT IS IMPOSSIBLE. BUT
WITH GOD EVERYTHING IS POSSIBLE.'"

MATTHEW 19:26

"NOW ALL GLORY TO GOD, WHO IS ABLE, THROUGH HIS
MIGHTY POWER AT WORK WITHIN US, TO ACCOMPLISH
INFINITELY MORE THAN WE MIGHT ASK OR THINK."

EPHESIANS 3:20

My God is Father, Protector, Counselor, and Lover of my soul. He is a Gentle Shepherd and Sacrificial Lamb. My God is all-mighty, all-powerful, all-knowing. He has power, He is power, and He shares power with believers.

Truly, there is none like You. Draw me closer every day. I lean into Your embrace and yield to Your ways. More than anything, I want to live a life that honors You.

I pause in my praise. I smile as I realize…

God used the annoyance of gnats to lead me into worship of Him. Oh, how He continues to bless and amaze me!

Reflections

Have you ever followed a spiritual "rabbit trail" right into a blessing? That's what my morning study felt like! Maintain a soft spirit and stay in the Word—He will lead you through beautiful encounters with Him!

It seems to me that people often look for an emotional experience with the Lord—but for me, the emotions come with understanding. He gives me joy and excitement and peace when He reveals the truth in this Love Story. How do you most often experience God's presence and leading?

Can you add a scripture verse to the list I found in my study?

9

· AN UNDIVIDED HEART ·

CONTEXT: *Joshua 24*

"SO FEAR THE LORD AND SERVE HIM
WHOLEHEARTEDLY." JOSHUA 24:14

I am sweeping the concrete pad in front of the run-in. It's a hot and lazy summer day. The wooden broom handle is warm in my hands and sweat drips from my brow. The *swish-swish* of the natural corn bristles moving across the unyielding surface joins the sweet quacks, chirps, and bleats of the animals around me. An occasional billowy, white cloud blocks the sun, fashioning a heavenly awning, a respite of shade and a moment of relief. The barn fan whirs continuously, producing a low-pitched, mechanical hum. No rest for weary fan blades in this heat.

I still my broom and watch my girls. The pasture hay is dry and thin but tall. The goats move slowly through the grasses disturbing a healthy population of late summer grasshoppers, crickets, and butterflies. The ducks and chickens are following the goats. The herd moves as one.

The grasshoppers leap away from the nibbling browsers and the ducks come in like raptors to scoop the insects into their bills and bellies. The chickens flap their wings with all their might trying to lift their plump bodies high enough to grab a bouncy treat. I laugh as the ducks pivot, reach, and celebrate each prize with a loud "Got 'em" quack. An individual barn swallow glides gracefully into the fray and picks up her own tasty meal.

I can't describe the pasture choreography as elegant or graceful. It is, however, very entertaining. It is also a productive routine. All the twists and twirls, jumps and lunges, yield a feast for my feathered friends. The meandering goats unwittingly provide the pace and tempo for the ensemble. It all comes together as a flourishing farm symphony should.

As I reflect on the teamwork displayed by the animals engaged in their natural behaviors, I see how obedience can extend beyond an action in response to a call. I think it also includes honoring the unique way in which we are designed. The Hebrew people of Old Testament times used one word, *avodah*, to refer to work, service, and worship. These three actions are united by one purpose:

"BUT AS FOR ME AND MY HOUSE, WE WILL SERVE (WORK AND WORSHIP) THE LORD."

JOSHUA 24:15 (KJV)

Serving is worship.

Serving the body of Christ, in the manner with which we are personally and preciously created, will certainly bring glory to God! His plan is always right. His plan is always good. When we align ourselves with His plan, the body functions as He intended. The goats nibble the grass and disturb the insects—allowing the birds to grab the bugs and fill their bellies. Healthy ducks and chickens lay delicious eggs—which fill my belly. We reap blessings as we honor God in worship through our service.

We honor God and His creation by applying our gifts and strengths in service—as we are uniquely equipped.

I appreciate the Hebrew word shama,10 which means to hear and obey. Shama is the expectation of a "Yes, Lord" response to God's instructions. I wonder if there is a Hebrew word for "hear and be." In a culture that allows us to choose even our gender, how do we learn to understand and magnify who God designed us to be? We are God's workmanship, His poetry—His work of art. We honor Him (and help others) by living the life He created us for.

I am not a beautiful, brave, and resourceful queen. However, like Queen Esther, I am called for my own "such a time as this"—and so are you, my friend. How do we discover more of our potential and discern our own specific godly assignments? I think it is simply a matter of participation. Being available goes a long way toward building the kingdom of heaven.

No matter how quirky or clumsy our efforts (or perhaps precisely because of those things!), we "become" when we "belong." When we are an active part of a godly community, we stretch our wings, we grow our hearts, we develop our skills, and we employ our passions—and in this process, we discover more about God and increasingly more about our role in His family.

Am I available? There is a well-known economic principle that states that 20 percent of the people do 80 percent of the work. If applied to our church organizations, that means that generally speaking, 80 percent of the body of Christ is passive when it comes to church service. No one can meet his or her potential from the sidelines. We will never meet our God-given potential by watching others work (serve and worship).

God wants me to be all in. His Word teaches me to love Him with all my heart, mind, soul, and strength (Deuteronomy 6:5). This is a call to action, not to spectating. Blessings flow from God who created me (and you!) to play a part.

What if we all approached God with the "Here I am" heart posture of Samuel (1 Samuel 3:4), Moses (Exodus

---

10 James Strong, *The New Strong's Expanded Exhaustive Concordance of the Bible*, Red letter ed. (Nashville: Thomas Nelson, 2010, 8085.

3:4), and Abraham (Genesis 22:1)? Here I am. I'm listening. I'm ready. I am eager to work, to serve, and to worship.

What if we stopped elevating Pinterest-perfect expectations over honest, best efforts as our standard? Here I am. I am ready to try. I am ready to open my heart, share my resources, and encourage someone. I am ready to do, to give, and to grow. I am Team Jesus, and I'm ready to play!

Reflections

"The master was full of praise. 'Well done, my good and faithful servant. You have been faithful in handling this small amount, so now I will give you many more responsibilities. Let's celebrate together!'" (Matthew 25:21)

I want to hear these words! I am sure that you do too. Does this verse motivate you? Why or why not?

Are you all in? The phrase "make every effort" is used nine times in the New Testament to refer to what we should give our best efforts toward. Four of these verses are written by Peter, the "Rock," a wonderful example of specific assignment based on his unique, imperfect personality as a Spirit-filled, transformed believer.

MAKE EVERY EFFORT:

2 Peter 1:5–8: to grow (add to) your faith

Hebrews 12:14: to live in peace with everyone

Luke 13:24: to enter through the narrow door

Romans 14:19: to do what leads to peace and mutual edification

Ephesians 4:3: to keep the unity of the Spirit

Hebrews 4:11: to enter into rest

2 Peter 1:10: to confirm your calling

2 Peter 1:15: to remember my teaching

2 Peter 3:14: to be found spotless, blameless, and at peace with him

Ask the Lord to focus your effort in one of these areas. What is He telling you?

10

✧ · ON MY KNEES · ✧

CONTEXT: *Romans 6*

"SIN IS NO LONGER YOUR MASTER...YOU LIVE
UNDER THE FREEDOM OF GRACE." ROMANS 6:14

FOUR GOATS STAND head-to-head-to-head-to-head near the barn. Heads are bowed with foreheads touching in the center of the group. Their bodies extend outward like petals on a pinwheel. I stop what I'm doing to watch them. I have no idea what they are doing or why they are positioned in this unusual way.

Eve, Lacey, Molly, and Meg—what are you up to, silly girls? I look more closely. The most curious thing about the behavior is the particular goats engaged in it.

Each goat in my herd has a distinctive personality. They are bonded in tight family groupings. These four goats generally tolerate one another but are not BFFs. Eve's tribe is Eleanor and Fern. Lacey and Meg are bound to Allie and Grace. Molly's besties are Maddie and Mai Tai. This precious pinwheel represents a doe from each "tribe" and I wonder what the G-4 (Goat-four) Summit is about?

Goats are enthusiastic head-butting professionals, but this is not head-butting. This is gentle, humble, affectionate behavior. These are goats from different family groups, simply being sweet together. They move ever so slowly around the circle, as if a gentle wind is pushing this fluffy goat whirligig.

There is a suggestion of carefree simplicity in the pinwheel, a humble spinning toy. I look at my goats through that filter. They are just being goats. Not a care in their world. Their feeders are full. The weather is pleasant and they are willing to give some attention to someone other than their best friend today. I feel their contentment and I consider a hospitable heart posture of my own.

We are called to give attention to one another—to people in need, who are outside of our typical social circles. There are endless opportunities to show interest, kindness, even hospitality to those who are not part of our inner circle. This is a command that continues to challenge me. I leave the goats and finish my chores while my thoughts linger on creative ways to share God's blessings of love, grace, and kindness with others.

Back inside, I use my search engine to locate Bible verses about hospitality and kindness. There are dozens highlighted on my screen, but a few prick my heart. I find Luke 14:12–14 in my NLT study Bible:

"Then he [Jesus] turned to his host, 'When you put on a luncheon or a banquet,' he said, 'don't invite your friends, brothers, relatives, and rich neighbors. For they will invite you back, and that will be your only reward. Instead, invite the poor, the crippled, the lame, and the blind. Then at the resurrection of the righteous, God will reward you for inviting those who could not repay you.'"

Jesus asks us to do some very hard things.

The kingdom of God looks nothing like the tiny kingdoms people have built on this earth. I have my own personal "kingdom." I have my family, friends, and ministries. It is all based on what I know, what I like, and what is comfortable. Jesus reaches out to *all*—but most especially to the lost, the forgotten, the marginalized, the poor, the grieved. But do *I* do this? Am I so wrapped up in my own self that I cannot graciously and generously extend my time and attention to a wounded soul? *Oh, Lord, redirect my heart.*

I see more and more people measuring their value by social media indicators. Even the term "social" media should alert us that we are looking at the wrong standard. We are putting ourselves under social pressure. It's like re-living middle school every day. We show off the selves we have created to look perfect. We compare ourselves to other fabricated profiles. We elevate celebrities, politicians, and possessions as saviors and idols. As I consider our worldly culture, I hear, "Father forgive them, for they know not what they do." But we should know. God's commands teach us to know better. His Spirit guides us to be better. How is it that we have collapsed into the arms of a godless, me-first culture?

And then I think of the word *humility.*

The Spirit illuminates the theme of humility, of dying to self. This is the lesson He is showing me and challenging me with repeatedly during this season. Pride blocks the work of the Spirit of God. I am eager to know Him more, to serve Him well, and to become the woman He wants me to be. He breaks my grip on control and independence by showing me what it is to be humble.

A simple breath of wind turns the petals on a pinwheel. God's breath is Spirit, *Pneuma* in Greek, *Ruach* in Hebrew. I am the petal. *Breathe on me. Be my motivation, my inclination, and my affection. On my knees and in awe of You, I soak in Your Word.*

I close my eyes and wait. He whispers.

A humble heart allows even the smallest holy breath to motivate our steps. I yield. I yield to the breath of God who loves me in spite of myself. I yield to Jesus, who gave His life in the greatest act of humble grace. I open my heart and hands, like the pinwheel petals, to be moved and to be used for His glory. I tell Him, "I am Yours."

Reflections

Transformation is the work of the Holy Spirit but He requires our permission, our cooperation, in the process. Ask Jesus to bring to your awareness any offense or misunderstanding. Let Him guide you to truth as you yield to the process. Has He shown you anything new today?

Consider the verses provided below from the English Standard Version. Look them up in a variety of translations. Compare the words from each. As you do, note in the margin of your Bible the words here or from other translations that pierce your heart and convict your soul.

"For all that is in the world—the desires of the flesh and the desires of the eyes and pride of life—is not from the Father but is from the world."
1 John 2:16

"Do nothing from selfish ambition or conceit, but in humility count others more significant than yourselves."
Philippians 2:3

"'Let the one who boasts, boast in the Lord.' For it is not the one who commends himself who is approved, but the one whom the Lord commends."
2 Corinthians 10:17–18.

"In the pride of his face the wicked does not seek him; all his thoughts are, 'There is no God.'"
Psalm 10:4

"I have been crucified with Christ. It is no longer I who live, but Christ who lives in me. And the life I now live in the flesh I live by faith in the Son of God, who loved me and gave himself for me."
Galatians 2:20

Has God whispered to you today? Write out your response to Him. Don't forget to add today's date.

11

❧ · HOLY HUMILITY · ❧

CONTEXT: *Ephesians 3*

"THEN CHRIST WILL MAKE HIS HOME IN
YOUR HEARTS AS YOU TRUST IN HIM. YOUR
ROOTS WILL GROW DOWN INTO GOD'S LOVE
AND KEEP YOU STRONG." EPHESIANS 3:17

THE AIR REMAINS warm and muggy—but there are still undeniable signs that autumn is creeping ever closer. Ducks and chickens molt annually. Shedding and growing new feathers is an important part of their health and survival. The timing of the molt depends on the age and breed of the bird. My ducks molt in late summer. My chickens start to shed about the same time and continue into the early fall.

Entering the pasture this time of year is like stepping into a pillow fight—feathers are scattered all over. There are feathers on the ground, in the nests, on the paths, in the water buckets, and on the dog. There are soft, white duck feathers everywhere I look. The first time I experienced this, I frantically counted poultry heads, certain that someone was missing!

The feathers don't fall out all at once. I do not have a farm full of naked birds during the molt. They shed and regrow feathers throughout the molting season. It is more like having a month of bad hair days. While I no longer panic, I still pay attention when bald spots show up on my beautiful girls. Bravo the Runner duck and Squirt, my chicken, were the first to start dropping their feathers this season.

Bravo's colors are white and fawn. I did a double take when she greeted me this morning. She looked terrible. I picked her up to get a closer look and to be certain that she wasn't sick. Nope. Not sick, no disease, no problem—just starting her molt. *I'm sorry Bravo*, I thought. *It will get worse before it gets better.* It is a good thing there are no mirrors hanging in the duck house!

Squirt was up on her shelf waiting for me to bring her breakfast. I could see that she was short a few tail feathers. This is an unfortunate look for little Squirt. This beautiful black Rosecomb hen is a heritage (historic) breed. She has silky black tail feathers that typically spread high above her head. She is a petite but proud chicken. Except today—today she looks a little ridiculous with one lonely tail feather waiting to drop from her bald bum.

There is something humbling about looking silly, sloppy, or sickly. We generally pride ourselves in a neat and attractive appearance. We feel more confident when we are dressed well. We feel more acceptable when makeup covers our flawed faces. Bravo and Squirt would not win any beauty pageants today. I think Squirt knew her tail feathers were gone—she didn't come off her shelf all morning.

God is holding me here in this study of humility, presenting more opportunities for me to learn. The power of transformation comes with the power to stay (remain, abide). I wait patiently for God to work. I hold on tight while He shows me a new way—His perfect, upside-down Way. While the world celebrates the proud, God embraces the humble.

Sometimes I make up my own studies. This is what I choose to do today. I write the word "humility" in my journal. Lingering over each letter, I engage. I explore. His Word is my map, my guide, my questions and my answers. Spirit to spirit, I consider what it takes to have a humble heart.

H = Holy Intervention.

There is no other way. Human willpower and discipline is not enough to overcome a natural predisposition for selfishness and pride. It is not enough to understand that "with God all things are possible" (Matthew 19:26), but also to know that it is *impossible* to live a faithful, humble life without divine empowerment. (Ephesians 3:20; Jeremiah 32:17)

U = Unconditional Grace.

Until we have received His heavenly grace, we cannot give it away. Now, because we have received this gift, we are overwhelmed with gratitude and His precious grace overflows from us. Humility starts by recognizing our own emptiness and allowing the streams of His goodness and grace to fill us up! Grace, like forgiveness, can be given precisely because it has been received. (Ephesians 4:31–32)

M = Measure of Faith.

Humility is a measure of spiritual maturity. As our faith grows, so does our character and our behavior. We reflect more of Christ as we grow our roots deep in Him. The fruit of the Spirit (evidence of our faith) flourish in a humble heart. (Ephesians 4:14–15; 1 Corinthians 13:11; 2 Peter 1:5–10)

I = "Not I, but Christ in me"

(Die to self; He must increase) (Galatians 2:20).

L = Love Lifts Up.

Love inspires and encourages. Humility requires holy love. Christ-followers are called to and recognized by their love for one another. "Your love for one another will prove to the world that you are my disciples" (John 13:35). Love in action is humble service to one another. (Hebrews 13:1–2; Galatians 5:13)

I = Intentional Obedience.

Those holy whispers are sent from heaven for a devoted *shama* (hear and obey) response. Be ready. Be willing. Be the watchman on the wall, looking out for opportunities to join the Lord in His work here on earth. When doubt threatens my effort, I think of Christ's obedience—He obeyed the will of the Father to the point of death on a cross (Philippians 2:8). There is no greater sacrifice that I can offer than what He has already done for me. His humble obedience is my motivation.

T = Tenderhearted Spirit.

"Since God chose you to be the holy people he loves, you must clothe yourselves with tenderhearted mercy" (Colossians 3:12). Humility requires and develops a soft heart toward others. In humility, we wrap vulnerability with tender care, the love of Jesus, and divine compassion. Mother Teresa, perhaps the greatest role model of tenderness since Jesus, is known for saying, "I don't do great things. I do small things with great love." I think she got that right. (1 Peter 3:8; Galatians 3:28)

Y = (His) Yoke Brings Rest.

Humble service can be exhausting, but union with Christ means we are never alone. When we are aligned with His will, He will equip and strengthen us for service. (Matthew 11:28–30; Isaiah 40:31)

Lord Jesus, I ask for Your mercy and grace—keep me humble and eager to love well, to live with purpose, and to honor You always.

Reflections

Do you have anything to add to the study of humility—a personal story or an inspirational verse? A new realization? Write it out on the next page.

Look up the verses highlighted in the devotional. Which of these verses provided further insight for you? What specifically did you see?

Consider the words of Abraham, father of our faith:

"ABRAHAM ANSWERED AND SAID, 'BEHOLD, I HAVE UNDERTAKEN TO SPEAK TO THE LORD, I WHO AM BUT DUST AND ASHES.'"
GENESIS 18:27 ESV

How would you describe the posture in which you speak to the Lord? Does your tone or spirit need any adjustment?

12

✌ · THE POWER OF WEAKNESS · ✌

CONTEXT: *2 Corinthians*

"PREACH THE WORD OF GOD. BE PREPARED,
WHETHER THE TIME IS FAVORABLE OR
NOT. PATIENTLY CORRECT, REBUKE,
AND ENCOURAGE YOUR PEOPLE WITH
GOOD TEACHING." 2 TIMOTHY 4:2

NOTHING STAYS THE SAME. Like everything else, our animals are demonstrating predictable effects of the passage of time. We moved to Shepherd's Gate ten years ago. Ten years may be a blink in eternity—but to an animal whose lifespan is a decade or two tops, ten years is most of their life.

Luna is fourteen years old. She is the largest and the oldest goat in our herd. I am often asked how long goats live. My heart answers, "not long enough." The researched response is that a healthy, well-cared-for Nigerian Dwarf goat lives an average of fifteen years. Bucks live closer to ten years. The stress of seasonal "rut" shortens the life span of the male.

Let me tell you about my Luna. Our dear Luna is the queen of the herd. She earned her place and the respect among the smaller, gentler goats by taking charge. She is the boss, the leader, and the judge. She is at the front of the line for affection and food. She settles arguments and leads the herd to graze. She is sweet and loving, bold and fearless, all at the same time. She has the strongest personality and the biggest heart of our herd.

Luna's full name is "Luna-tic." She earned that name as a kid because of her high energy and demanding temperament. Luna demanded attention. She would leap over all the other kids to be first to the bottle or first onto a lap to be cuddled. As she grew, she consistently butted anyone competing for the food bowl. This girl had boundless energy and was full of confidence. She was the source of constant giggles and hours of snuggles.

I remember delivering her kids several years ago. She labored long into the night. I sat in the hay with her for hours stroking her soft neck and praying. She would rest her head on my lap between contractions, breathing slowly and calmly. She never seemed worried. She was sure, resolute, and focused. She delivered two of the most beautiful babies I have ever seen into my waiting hands.

There was a shift in the herd over the long winter. Luna entered spring with an arthritic limp. When the dormant pasture grasses grew lush and green again, inviting the goats to browse, it was not Luna leading the herd out. These days, my Luna often lags behind the group, or stays in the barn to rest. Today, I watched Luna stand away from the food trough to avoid all the pushing and shoving that goes on around the grain.

My Luna is neither as strong nor as able as she once was. I would even say that she is vulnerable now—and she seems to know it. The younger goats are selecting their new boss. It's not clear yet who will take charge, but Luna will soon need to relinquish her crown. This is how it goes in the animal world. The spiritual world is different.

The apostle Paul's ministry was periodically marked by doubters and critics regarding his authority. Paul responded to people who considered him weak, meek, or timid (depending on your translation) in 2 Corinthians 10. Paul wrote the letter that we call 2 Corinthians when he was in a vulnerable place in his ministry. He sent a young Timothy out to various locations while he, Paul, continued to teach the growing body of Christ through his writing. Second Corinthians is a personal and heartfelt letter that, among many other things, reflects Paul's struggles and weaknesses. Paul wrote of the "thorn in his side" that God refused to remove (2 Corinthians 12) and repeatedly defended his authority to teach.

Paul's response to his personal challenges and to his challengers is eloquently summarized in chapter 12, verses 9–10. I look it up in my NLT Study Bible:

"[JESUS] SAID, 'MY GRACE IS ALL YOU NEED. MY POWER WORKS BEST IN WEAKNESS.' SO NOW I [PAUL]

AM GLAD TO BOAST ABOUT MY WEAKNESSES, SO THAT THE POWER OF CHRIST CAN WORK THROUGH ME. THAT'S WHY I TAKE PLEASURE IN MY WEAKNESSES, AND IN THE INSULTS, HARDSHIPS, PERSECUTIONS, AND TROUBLES THAT I SUFFER FOR CHRIST. FOR WHEN I AM WEAK, THEN I AM STRONG."

The last word in that text is "strong," or "*dunatos*"[11] in the Greek. It means strong, powerful, or able. It also has a spiritual indication of being strong in soul, firm in conviction or faith.

I pause here. I understand what Paul is teaching but I want my spirit to soak it all in. Like Luna, I am growing weaker with age. "Seniors" are not necessarily valued or respected in our American culture like they are in others. I find myself feeling insecure about what I have to offer the younger generations. I wonder why, in my mid-fifties, I am eager to start a new career in writing and publishing. Ideas like, "Who do I think I am?" and, "It's way too late for me now" swirl around in my brain.

And yet, God continually calls me to write, to share, to teach. The more I lean on Him, the more I want to do what I believe He has designed me to do. I may not have decades in front of me, but I want every single day to count for Christ. He calls each one of us to an assignment. We have to trust that He knows exactly what He is doing. The more incapable I feel, the more I depend on Him. I think it's supposed to work that way. For if I can do it without God's help, is He really in it—or am I just full of myself?

God's power works best in my weakness. It's not about my success; it's about His glory. He will continue to use the weak, the meek, and the timid to point people to Himself. I am so thankful that He (still) wants to use me to encourage and grow His family.

Thank You, Jesus, for the example of those who have gone before us and for the wisdom found in Your Word. I pray that You would cover any "seniors" reading these words today with Your grace and confidence to persevere in any and every small way. Let them know how valuable they (still) are!

---

11 James Strong, *The New Strong's Expanded Exhaustive Concordance of the Bible*, Red letter ed. (Nashville: Thomas Nelson, 2010), 1415.

Reflections

At the end of Paul's life and ministry, he wrote to encourage his student Timothy. Read chapter 4 of 2 Timothy for a heart-felt view of a man who had poured out his whole life as an offering to God. He used himself up to the last drop in service for Christ. He is a wonderful example of what it is like to live "all in," fully devoted, wholly given to the Lord. How does Paul's example influence your perspective?

Our days are numbered and our age is irrelevant to Christ. Reflect on the verses below and write out your thoughts and prayer on the next page.

"THE GLORY OF THE YOUNG IS THEIR STRENGTH; THE GRAY HAIR OF EXPERIENCE IS THE SPLENDOR OF THE OLD."

PROVERBS 20:29

"TEACH US TO REALIZE THE BREVITY OF LIFE, SO THAT WE MAY GROW IN WISDOM."

PSALM 90:12

Fall

THIS IS THE SEASON WHEN CANADIAN GEESE CAPTURE OUR

GAZE IN THEIR PROFICIENT V FLYING FORMATIONS, WOOLLY

BEAR CATERPILLARS SCURRY FOR SHELTER, COLORFUL

LEAVES FLOAT SILENTLY TO THE GROUND, AND CARVED

PUMPKINS DECORATE FRONT PORCHES.

———————

STAY ON TARGET

CONTENTS: *Ephesians 1*

"AND THIS IS THE PLAN: AT THE RIGHT TIME HE WILL BRING EVERYTHING TOGETHER UNDER THE AUTHORITY OF CHRIST—EVERYTHING IN HEAVEN AND ON EARTH." EPHESIANS 1:10

———

I NEED A SWEATSHIRT this morning. I pull it on over my head as I step outside. My feet know the way and I walk to the pasture on autopilot before my morning coffee. The dew is heavy and the grass soaks my boots. The soft, wet autumn grass yields with a pleasant *swish-swish* instead of the dry *crunch-crunch* of summer. On the other side of the gate, more than a dozen eyes shine (shades of blue, brown, amber, and nearly black), tails wag (short, perky tails; long, feathered tails; and one extra-excited, fluffy tail), ducks honk, and a single proud rooster crows. Everyone is up out of bed and eager for breakfast—everyone except Luna.

My sweet Luna. My oldest, snuggliest, spoiled girl. She is still in her cozy hay bed, like a queen, waiting for me to greet her. And I do, of course. I bow down and stroke her soft head. "Good morning, my girl." She lifts her head and her amber eyes meet mine.

Luna has earned her right to sleep in. Her arthritic limbs need a little extra time in the forgiving bedding. I smile at her as I think of us as two "old goats" sharing the morning rhythm and the effects of an aging body.

After I feed everyone else, Luna comes to the door of the tack room where she receives her special bowl of extruded hay pellets. While she eats, I massage her head and neck and that stiff right front leg. When she swallows her last bite, Luna sighs and leans her head on my chest. I want to stay right here, in this moment. The warmth of Luna's body and the silkiness of her fur between my fingers is a covering of peace and comfort. I don't want to move. I stay as long as I can before I go out and finish my chores.

Like Luna, I am a slow mover in the morning. My obligations can overwhelm me. The thought of canceling my day to stay home with my animals comes to my mind. I think it would be so much easier to let everything go and just enjoy my day. Never mind what anyone else needs today. Never mind writing books… planning lessons… running errands…never mind answering messages… making meals… more meetings and assignments. Just never mind.

I think about it, but I don't do that today. I don't "never mind" anything. *Grumpy Monkey*–my grandson's favorite children's story—pops into my head. I think of three-year-old Josh's best imitation of the monkey's voice as he says, "I'm not grumpy!" I smile ear to ear and decide to start my lesson plan for my Friday morning Bible study group. *Thank You, Lord, for my grandson and happy memories to motivate and encourage me.*

Our group agreed to read and study Ephesians together. I set out my Bibles, a commentary, my notebook, and some colored pens. I love being surrounded by books. Finally, I pour my coffee. I am consistently moved to giving thanks for this precious first cup of steaming morning brew. *Thank You, Lord, for creating coffee and for the pleasure it brings.* The aroma alone awakens my senses. My mood is lifted and I'm feeling more motivated already.

I start every Bible study with a background check, so to speak. I am eager to learn the historical context that gives me clues and imagery about the content, the period, and the author. Before I read the holy Scriptures, I read about who wrote it, where, when, and why. My study Bible, commentary, and Internet search engine all help me with this process.

As I open my mind to what surrounds the book of Ephesians, written by the apostle Paul nearly thirty years after Jesus' death and resurrection, I am reminded that this missive was one among many of the so-called prison epistles (letters Paul wrote while in prison for preaching the gospel). I pause already. Paul was put in prison multiple times during his teaching ministry. Paul was beaten, stoned, and expelled from towns and communities while being faithful to God's assignment to share the good news, the gospel of Christ Jesus. Pause. Stop.

I meditate, not in a peaceful, blissful moment, but in a moment of honor, respect, and conviction. Paul truly yielded his whole being to the work God gave him to do, nothing left in reserve. Paul lived faithfully according to his God-given calling.

Paul wrote the letter to the church in Ephesus while he was a prisoner of Rome—but considered himself a captive servant to Jesus.

"PAUL, A SERVANT OF CHRIST JESUS, CALLED TO BE AN APOSTLE, SET APART FOR THE GOSPEL OF GOD."

ROMANS 1:1 ESV

He continued to share the gospel in prison, in a pagan capital, and in hostile circumstances. He shared the gospel with enthusiastic confidence, unwavering purpose, and unshakable truth. What a contrast to our current culture, where comfort places first and security second on a list of idols worshiped by modern-day Christians.[12] While we crave and covet our comforts, Paul suffered—truly suffered—for Christ.

---

12 Marissa Postell, "Pastors Identify Modern-Day Idols," *Lifeway Research*, August 9, 2022.

Paul's purpose was to share the good news, the gospel message of Christ, with anyone who would listen. He aspired to encourage and equip believers to mature in their faith through discipleship in simple home churches. I imagine that Paul was passionately focused on the assignment in front of him, and nothing else.

I don't think that being imprisoned was part of Paul's plan, and yet, it was clearly part of God's plan. The letters Paul wrote to the churches, communities, and people during his time in prison are what we now call books. Paul wrote thirteen out of the twenty-seven books in the New Testament. This faithful apostle contributed nearly half of all the works we rely on to understand the Christian faith and life.

If Paul had not been incarcerated, would he have written those letters? If Paul had followed his plan, he might well have spoken to those churches and people in person. He would have shared time, meals, and conversations with people. He surely would have encouraged that community of believers in that time. Instead, God allowed Paul to sit quietly in chains, where, with the help of the Holy Spirit, the letters that have guided and grown generations of believers were penned.

Nothing left in reserve: Paul, like the disciples, gave his life for his ministry and mission to love and serve Jesus. Not long before his execution, Paul wrote to encourage his dear friend Timothy: "I have fought the good fight, I have finished the race, I have kept the faith." (2 Timothy 4:7 NIV). He stayed faithful to the assignment right in front of him. Like Moses, Abraham, and so many others, Paul left this earth without seeing God's promises fulfilled. Paul never knew how far and how wide his letter-writing campaign would reach. I pause again and take it in.

This perspective lifts the veil of self-centered, comfort-seeking idolatry for me. Conviction settles into my soul. Teaching the children, leading the Bible studies, writing the book, showing kindness to a stranger, and preparing meals are simple tasks. I won't know how my faithfulness will impact others—but I stay the course anyway. *Thank You, Lord, for simple assignments. Thank You for allowing me to serve, here and now.* God has so much more for us than what we can see—and yet, that is exactly where He needs our focus. He will do the rest. *Thank You, Lord.*

Reflections

What are you committed to today or tomorrow? (Consider your schedule, your to-do list.)

Where is God on your list of things to do and people to serve?

Keeping God on our list is an important, intentional step in keeping our life and priorities on target. How do you keep yourself motivated to stay in the Word and faithful in prayer?

Paul planned to travel, but God said to stay put. Can you think of a time when God directed your path differently than your own thoughtful plan?

On the next page, write or share about God's clear direction and what you learned from that experience.

2

THE HEART OF REMEMBERING

CONTEXT: *Psalm 103* AND *105:1-8*

"LET ALL THAT I AM PRAISE THE LORD;
MAY I NEVER FORGET THE GOOD THINGS
HE DOES FOR ME." PSALM 103:2

NOTHING SAYS FALL is in the air quite like the fabulous aroma of pumpkin spice. Lemon flavors move off the shelves to make room for the avalanche of pumpkin spice goodies. Baked goods, coffees, creamers, icings, ice cream, cereals, syrups, candles, room sprays, and oils—all bursting with the delicious cinnamony-pumpkin aromas we associate with the onset of fall. Yum! Unless you live on a goat farm, where bucks in rut take autumn scents to a completely different place! Not yum.

Early fall heralds breeding season for the dairy goat farmer. If I want that wonderful, fresh goat milk in the spring, I have to breed my does in the fall. The Nigerian Dwarf goat gestation period is five months (145 to 150 days). A healthy doe typically delivers one to three kids.

We have even had several quadruplets delivered at Shepherd's Gate. Captain Jack and Sergeant Pepper are our studs. They have eagerly performed their studly duties and produced several generations of goats.

It is impossible to forget breeding season. The male goats (bucks) never forget. Their biology kicks in this time of year and they break out that uniquely sour-musky, buck cologne that drives the lady goats wild. Some people describe the bucks-in-rut smell like a dog sprayed by a skunk. Yes, it's that lovely. All I have to do is get near the bucks and that putrid smell sticks to me. I have to change clothes every time I step into their pen between September and December.

The clear skies and gentle breezes waft the stink over to the girls' pen and alert them that the eligible bachelors are ready and waiting. The boys splash on their manly scent and the girls wag and lift their tails. That's about all it takes. It amazes me how something that smells that awful to me is like Giorgio Armani to my precious girls.

Strong reminders of a season help us to stay faithful to our purpose and calling. The Hebrew people developed traditions and built monuments to help them remember God's protection. They had words (rules) carved into stone, and they held feasts and festivals to celebrate God's provision. They erected stone towers and passed stories down from one generation to the next. They kept a divine record of God's holy work and words.

Remembrance invites thanks. Remembrance inspires courage. Remembrance develops faith. Remembrance honors an omnipotent God who saves. Thousands of years ago, King David wrote about remembering:

"I REMEMBER THE DAYS OF OLD. I PONDER ALL YOUR GREAT WORKS AND THINK ABOUT WHAT YOU HAVE DONE. I LIFT MY HANDS TO YOU IN PRAYER. I THIRST FOR YOU AS PARCHED LAND THIRSTS FOR RAIN."

PSALM 143:5–6

The beauty of God's living Word is that it speaks to us even today. We are called to remember. The power of remembrance floods my heart and soul with joy. God's gift of happy, blessed memories of days that are forever gone, but accessible in my mind, make me smile.

Volumes of scrapbooks and photo albums; colorful artwork created by small, uncoordinated hands; homemade, perfectly imperfect Christmas ornaments; the home run baseball; a pair of tiny ice skates; the soccer jersey that hangs on my wall—these are among my treasured memories of God's blessings. They represent not only my children and grandchildren but also the cherished time we shared together over the years, the investment in one another's lives, and the grace of God that binds us all.

Even though my children and grandchildren live far away, I can remember pushing them on swings, long walks on trails, a zillion art projects, meals, conversations, and games around the kitchen table, bubble baths and bedtime stories, and that irresistible sound of a child's giggle. I can remember teaching their Sunday school classes, worshiping side by side, countless hours cheering at practices, recitals, games, and competitions. I am overwhelmed with gratitude as I count every precious moment a gift from God.

Not all of our memories are happy. I understand that. I have unhappy memories too. But I don't dwell there. I don't live according to my past mistakes or disappointments. Remembering what God has done in previous seasons also means remembering that He has moved me out of that muck. Remembering who I was keeps me humble, for it is God's grace that rescued and changed me. He has pulled me out of more pits than I care to confess, and I don't want to crawl back in!

I am thankful for His provision. I am aware of His mercy. I honor Him by learning the lessons and moving ahead—toward whatever He has for me next. Moses taught the Hebrews:

"BE CAREFUL NOT TO FORGET THE LORD, WHO RESCUED YOU FROM SLAVERY IN THE LAND OF EGYPT."

DEUTERONOMY 6:12

This statement is past tense—leave your old self in the past. I have been rescued! And so have you. As believers, we are new creations in Christ (2 Corinthians 5:17; Ephesians 2:5).

As we mature in Christ, we continue to transform. Since this is a lifelong process, we want to maintain our forward trajectory. Honor God and His work by remembering how far you have come!

"He causes us to remember his wonderful works. How gracious and merciful is our LORD!" Psalm 111:4

With a heart that longs to honor God through remembrance, I want to share my acrostic for PRAY as you may find it helpful. I follow this pattern in my daily prayers:

P = Praise.

I start every prayer with a celebration of who He is!

R = Remember.

I recall what God has done for me in the last twenty-four hours. This is my gratitude time. I thank Him for His Presence, guidance, provision, and so on in very specific terms. I never want to overlook an opportunity to thank Him!

A = Ask.

I need divine assistance every day. I don't want to live a day without His Presence.

Y = Yield.

I posture my heart in "Yes, Lord" obedience to God's intervention, regardless of how He responds to my prayer.

Reflections

Write out the P-R-A-Y acrostic and follow the instructions for your own personal time in prayer with Him today.

Think about how far you have come as a believer and praise God for growing you up!

Don't believe the lie that your past defines you. You past does not dictate or define your future unless you believe that lie. How can you view your own mistakes, missteps, and sins as opportunities to learn, to grow, and to change? Can you think of some things you have learned, or changed, because of your past?

The acrostic P-R-A-Y is a strategy designed to help us remember what God has done for us and how to honor Him through prayer. Do you have any strategies that help you to remember important details or events—spiritual or otherwise?

How do you want to be remembered?

3

❧ · COLORS OF CHANGE · ❧

CONTEXT: *2 Corinthians 4:7-18*

"WE NOW HAVE THIS LIGHT SHINING IN
OUR HEARTS, BUT WE OURSELVES ARE
LIKE FRAGILE CLAY JARS CONTAINING THIS
GREAT TREASURE." 2 CORINTHIANS 4:7

FALL ROLLED IN right on time this year. No tiptoe to the starting line, no thought-ful hesitation, no delay. No lingering warm Indian summer to extend pool activities and picnics. Delightfully cool temperatures, air as fresh as the Honeycrisp apples ripe for harvest, gentle breezes, and the changing of colors on the trees came with a flip of the calendar's page.

The natural rhythms of the earth on display give me peace of mind. I twirl the stem of a maple leaf between my fingers. The contrast of the vivid red and gold holds my gaze. God is in control. In spite of what can feel like chaos all around us, His Spirit remains calm, confident, and peaceful. He has not relinquished power. He does not change. He has a plan and He stays solidly, immovably focused on His purpose.

As I reflect on Him today, I know that while God is my calm in the storm, my firm foundation, my strength and my song, He calls me to change, to grow, and to transform a little more every day. As the green leaves mutate to reds and golds, so must I yield to the seasons of change. Pressure that brings pain can also produce something beautiful.

Often, there is no other way. I have been here before, and so have you. We can't stop the seasons. We can't stop time, the advance of years, the sprouting of gray hair, or the appearance of those unwanted wrinkles. Our response to change matters.

God's immutability is my safety net. His constancy allows me to step out, season after season, even moment after moment, into the unknown. His Spirit guides my path. His light rarely shines more than a few steps ahead for me—but I step confidently forward because I trust Him. I can face the new season, whatever lies ahead, because He is with me.

How many times have I prayed and asked God to change an unpleasant, inconvenient, or painful situation? Over my lifetime, I couldn't begin to count those prayers. No one likes pain; no one enjoys the grieving process or even interruptions to their schedule. Our human response to pain is to avoid it. When we navigate through life, we look for the path of least resistance, the straightest road, the most efficient route—that is simple wisdom, isn't it?

"But God…" Spiritually speaking, we accept that God's ways often contradict basic human nature. He has led me smack into storms. He has allowed pain and death and loss to camp at my door. I don't understand it. I don't like it. So I pray it away: "God take this from me." But God did not take the cup from Jesus or the thorn from Paul. My faith tells me that God stayed true to His plan in spite of their pain. His divine plan for human redemption is not a clear and easily discernable path. We cannot imagine all the work that He does to make things right in the end. We just know that He will.

There are times when God grieves too. God grieves over evil that hurts His beloved. God takes no pleasure in our pain.

"THE LORD OBSERVED THE EXTENT OF HUMAN WICKEDNESS ON THE EARTH, AND HE SAW THAT

EVERYTHING THEY THOUGHT OR IMAGINED WAS CONSISTENTLY AND TOTALLY EVIL. SO THE LORD WAS SORRY HE EVER MADE THEM AND PUT THEM ON THE EARTH. IT BROKE HIS HEART."

GENESIS 6:5-6

This verse was written about five thousand years ago. It describes the broken heart of God in the time of Noah. But God stays faithful to His plan, His purposes, and His promises.

There is pain in my life that God allows to continue. I grow weary of it. Some days I can hardly stand it. I can only assume that this is an essential part of my transformation. He will stay with me until I am changed. The situation, the circumstance, may not change—but I will. He will give me the heart, the perspective, the strategies, and the strength I need to become more and more like Jesus. When I yield to His Spirit in obedience, He can truly work in and through me.

I turn the leaf in my hand again. The bright red, yellow, and purple hues are pretty. If the autumn sheds stay on the ground, they will dry out; the leaves will turn brown and blow away to mulch the forest floor over winter. I decide to gather some for pressing. I collect a dozen and bring them back inside. Between sheets of wax paper, and under heavy books, they will dry with their bright colors preserved. They will be an art project for another day.

I walk back to the house and I look up the words God gave Paul to encourage the church:

"I PRAY THAT FROM HIS GLORIOUS, UNLIMITED RESOURCES HE WILL

EMPOWER YOU WITH INNER STRENGTH THROUGH HIS SPIRIT. THEN CHRIST WILL MAKE HIS HOME IN YOUR HEARTS AS YOU TRUST IN HIM. YOUR ROOTS WILL GROW DOWN INTO GOD'S LOVE AND KEEP YOU STRONG. AND MAY YOU HAVE THE POWER TO UNDERSTAND, AS ALL GOD'S PEOPLE SHOULD, HOW WIDE, HOW LONG, HOW HIGH, AND HOW DEEP HIS LOVE IS. MAY YOU EXPERIENCE THE LOVE OF CHRIST, THOUGH IT IS TOO GREAT TO UNDERSTAND FULLY. THEN YOU WILL BE MADE COMPLETE WILL ALL THE FULLNESS OF LIFE AND POWER THAT COMES FROM GOD."

EPHESIANS 3:14-19

I use a fallen leaf as my bookmark and close my Bible here. Thank You, heavenly Father, for keeping me close through every season. Thank you for putting Your treasure in this humble, fragile jar of clay.

Reflections

God is immutable and omnipresent. These characteristics of God give me a great sense of peace and calm in any storm. What characteristics of God form your "safety net"?

What is your greatest source of comfort in difficult situations?

Do you think of yourself as fragile or strong in this season? Why?

How have your responses to disappointment and challenges changed over time?

What scripture verses help you to remember God's sovereignty and grace?

Listen to this song, "Surrounded," about God in the battle as you color the next page.

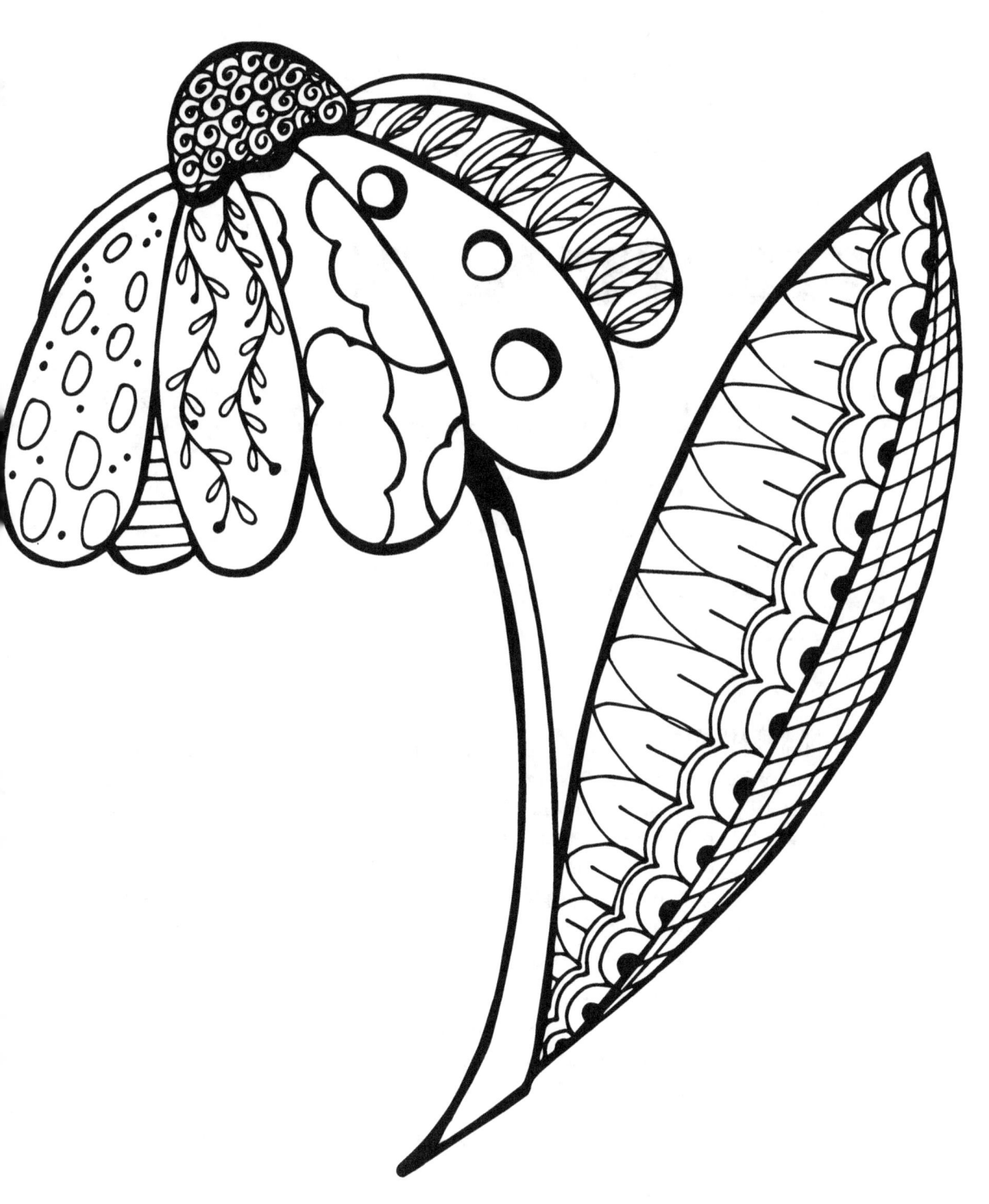

4

• TIME BY THE FIRE •

CONTEXT: *1 Chronicles 29:10-20*

"O LORD, THE GOD OF OUR ANCESTOR ISRAEL, MAY YOU BE PRAISED FOREVER AND EVER!" 1 CHRONICLES 29:10

IT SEEMS A little early—the first day of October—but cold is cold, so today I caved and lit a fire in the fireplace. First fire of the season. What is it about the warmth of a fire that totally changes my mood? With a fire glowing in the hearth, I am content to sit and read, to bake cookies, to write a letter, to sip a mug of spiced herbal tea…and all is well. Fires in the fireplace are a source of joy to me! Thank You, Lord, for the crackle of dry, old wood. Thank You for the pop of cinders and sparks that jump like tiny, personal fireworks cheering on the greater blaze. Thank You for the smell of cherry and walnut mingling in smoky tendrils leaving the chimney. Oh, just thank You, Lord!

It is a great day to give thanks. I decide this is the place to rest my spirit today— soaking in His blessings with a grateful heart. I carry my heavy study Bible, journal, and mug full of pens and markers to the kitchen island. I open the book to 1 Chronicles and find chapter 29, verses 10–20.

There is a prayer written here, a great prayer of David. His prayer is an eloquent reminder that all we are, all we have, and all we do is for the glory of God. He reminds us that God is to be praised and exalted above all else.

David's prayer, by itself, is a powerful example of humble gratitude. Taken in its context, however, it is an even more profound prayer. At this time in history, King David was preparing to pass his crown and the kingdom to his son Solomon.

Wealth and reminders of his successful reign surrounded David as king. He had every human reason to shine the spotlight and usurp glory for himself—but he did not. He had every reason to be distracted by the comfort and riches in his environment—but he did not.

He even had every reason to feel resentful and disappointed that he was not chosen by God to build the holy temple. It was one thing that God did not allow David to do. It would be Solomon, not his father, who would build the permanent temple for God in Jerusalem. (Just as it was Joshua, not Moses, who would finally step into the promised land with the next generation of God's people.) David counted it a blessing that his son would continue to serve God in that way. Not only did he have an incredible attitude, but David collected supplies, treasures, and craftsmen to help Solomon succeed.

King David honored the holy God of Israel and worshiped our mighty, loving, faithful God with great joy. I can feel his authentic worship and exaltation in his words. This prayer reveals King David's heart for God.

I read the scriptures, eleven verses, and then write them in my journal. I divide the prayer into four paragraphs to help me focus. I circle, underline, and highlight the words and phrases that stand out to me. I settle in and ask the Holy Spirit to help me see how I need to grow in my own prayer life.

VERSES 10–12:

"THEN DAVID PRAISED THE LORD IN THE PRESENCE OF THE WHOLE ASSEMBLY: 'OH LORD, THE GOD OF

OUR ANCESTOR ISRAEL, MAY YOU
BE PRAISED FOREVER AND EVER!
YOURS, O LORD, IS THE GREATNESS,
THE POWER, THE GLORY, THE
VICTORY, AND THE MAJESTY.
EVERYTHING IN HEAVEN AND ON
EARTH IS YOURS, O LORD, AND THIS
IS YOUR KINGDOM.

WE ADORE YOU AS THE ONE WHO
IS OVER ALL THINGS. WEALTH
AND HONOR COME FROM YOU
ALONE, FOR YOU RULE OVER
EVERYTHING. POWER AND MIGHT
ARE IN YOUR HAND, AND AT YOUR
DISCRETION PEOPLE ARE MADE
GREAT AND GIVEN STRENGTH."

I pick up my blue pen. I circle "praised the Lord" and underline "in the presence of the whole assembly." David led with confidence. He led by example. People see what we do.

I highlight "LORD" times 3 in yellow. The capital L-O-R-D is our English translation of the Hebrew word Yahweh—the proper and revered name of the eternal God who deserves our humble respect.

My blue pen circles "greatness," "power," "glory," "victory," and "majesty." When do I use words like this to honor my faithful, loving God?

I draw a red wiggly line under "Everything in heaven and on earth is yours." I acknowledge that truth now. I release the grip on my pride and my things. It is all Yours, dear heavenly Father. Don't let me forget!

I draw a green box around the phrase, "We adore you as the one who is over all things." I take a moment to adore Him.

VERSES 13–15:

"O OUR GOD, WE THANK YOU AND PRAISE YOUR GLORIOUS NAME! BUT WHO AM I, AND WHO ARE MY PEOPLE, THAT WE COULD GIVE ANYTHING TO YOU? EVERYTHING WE HAVE HAS COME FROM YOU, AND WE GIVE YOU ONLY WHAT YOU FIRST GAVE US! WE ARE HERE FOR ONLY A MOMENT, VISITORS AND STRANGERS IN THE LAND AS OUR ANCESTORS WERE BEFORE US. OUR DAYS ON EARTH ARE LIKE A PASSING SHADOW, GONE SO SOON WITHOUT A TRACE."

I highlight "our God" and know that it is translated from the Hebrew word, Elohim—which is also a Hebrew name of God. "Elohim" is our strong Creator God.

My blue pen circles "we thank you" and underlines "praise your glorious name." Names have meaning. I draw an arching arrow from this phrase to my highlighted "God."

I put a green box around the phrase "Everything we have has come from you." I close my eyes and give thanks for what He has given me. I think of my family, my education, and opportunities. I think of my skills and strengths, my weaknesses and faults. I think of time spent with the people I love, and I thank Him for it all.

VERSES 16–17:

"O LORD OUR GOD, EVEN THIS MATERIAL WE HAVE GATHERED TO BUILD A TEMPLE TO HONOR YOUR HOLY NAME COMES FROM YOU! IT ALL BELONGS TO

YOU! I KNOW, MY GOD, THAT
YOU EXAMINE OUR HEARTS
AND REJOICE WHEN YOU FIND
INTEGRITY THERE. YOU KNOW I
HAVE DONE ALL THIS WITH GOOD
MOTIVES, AND I HAVE WATCHED
YOUR PEOPLE OFFER THEIR GIFTS
WILLINGLY AND JOYOUSLY."

I highlight the first phrase, "O LORD our God." David is joyful in God's presence, pleased to say His name! He speaks with admiration and honor of the great, eternal, all-mighty Creator God as I might speak of my strong, handsome, wise husband!

I put a green box around the phrase "you examine our hearts and rejoice when you find integrity there." I pause and thank God for growing my heart and spirit—for calling me closer, for taking my heart of stone and giving me a heart of flesh (Ezekiel 36:26).

VERSES 18–20:

"O LORD THE GOD OF OUR
ANCESTORS ABRAHAM, ISAAC, AND
ISRAEL, MAKE YOUR PEOPLE ALWAYS
WANT TO OBEY YOU. SEE TO IT
THAT THEIR LOVE FOR YOU NEVER
CHANGES. GIVE MY SON SOLOMON
THE WHOLEHEARTED DESIRE
TO OBEY ALL YOUR COMMANDS,
LAWS, AND DECREES, AND TO DO

EVERYTHING NECESSARY TO BUILD
THIS TEMPLE, FOR WHICH I HAVE
MADE THESE PREPARATIONS.

THEN DAVID SAID TO THE WHOLE
ASSEMBLY, "GIVE PRAISE TO THE
LORD YOUR GOD!" AND THE WHOLE
ASSEMBLY PRAISED THE LORD,
THE GOD OF THEIR ANCESTORS,
AND THEY BOWED LOW AND KNELT
BEFORE THE LORD AND THE KING."

I highlight "O LORD the God…" and underline "Abraham, Isaac, and Israel." Our eternal, all-mighty Creator God is making a way for us! He is working through the generations to see it through. And through Jacob-Israel came the Lion of Judah! I am so thankful for God's patience!

I put a green box around the phrase "always want to obey you. See to it that their love for you never changes." This is a familiar prayer. Lord, prick my ears and let me hear. Let me hear and lovingly obey Your voice each day.

I am so thankful for David's awesome prayer. God, I praise You. I adore You. You are a great and powerful God! You are mighty and majestic! You give us victory over every battle! I am overwhelmed by Your love and grace! I review the words inside the green boxes again and pray over them quietly.

I cap my pens and close my journal. I am so grateful for time spent in His beautiful Word!

Reflections

How do you study and learn best? I love paper and pens and all colorful study tools. I like to read real books that I can highlight and write in. I like to learn from others by listening to Bible studies when I am driving, or podcasts on my phone, by watching video series and documentaries, and attending conferences and seminars. Do you know your learning style?

I am thankful that there are so many resources available to ready and study the Bible. I am more interested in reading the Bible today than ever before. God has given me a hunger for the Word. Not every season has been like this. I think the most challenging season for opening the Bible was when my children were young and dependent. What is your current season of life?

What are your challenges to securing study time? What method of study is most helpful to you in this season of your life?

What goals do you have for the next season?

5

CONTEXT: *Psalm 1*

"BUT THEY DELIGHT IN THE LAW OF THE LORD, MEDITATING ON IT DAY AND NIGHT. THEY ARE LIKE TREES PLANTED ALONG THE RIVERBANK, BEARING FRUIT EACH SEASON." PSALM 1:2–3

I COMPLETE FARM chores twice a day. Each morning, I carry hay from the barn to the shelter in the pasture. I fill the hay feeders with fresh, sweet-smelling orchard grass hay harvested from our fields during the summer months. The girls come to nibble the new grass as soon as it arrives even though they ate through the night. Some mornings I ask if they "approve this selection." They always do.

I empty water buckets, wipe them clean, and fill them with cool, clean water from the pump. I fill chicken bowls, duck bowls, and dog bowls with food and water. I spread grain in the goat trough. Luna and Fern receive their special portion by hand. I milk the does in season. We don't have any girls "in milk" currently, so that is one less thing to do right now.

Everyone who wants it gets a belly or head rub when I rest from my work. Everyone except for the boys in rut—they get a scratch from the end of a rake when they are in full stinky season. While the ducks do not generally enjoy being held or petted, they do love a good worm hunt. Five Indian Runner ducks will follow me from log to bucket

to rock waiting for me to turn them over and reveal a yum-my snack. They will even honk loudly (cheering me on, I'm sure) if I move too slowly or get distracted.

If I hurry, I can finish my chores relatively quickly. I rarely hurry. I enjoy my time with the animals, so I linger. My mom would say that I "dawdle." I repeat the same routine again in the evening. I am a little faster in the evening, only because I am trying to get our own dinner on the table too.

The pasture animals see me every morning and every evening. They greet me eagerly. They know their names. They trust me. Love and care spilled out generously over time engenders the knowing and trusting.

It has not always been easy to make time to read my Bible or journal my thoughts or sit quietly and wait for some perception of an answer to prayer. It's not "easy" now—but I can't help myself. I am compelled to seek Him. I am so very eager to spend time with Him, to sit in His Presence, to linger over His Word, and to know Him more. I look forward to the Spirit-to-spirit connection when He teaches me something new or reminds me of something precious.

"KEEP THIS BOOK OF THE LAW ALWAYS ON YOUR LIPS; MEDITATE ON IT DAY AND NIGHT, SO THAT YOU MAY BE CAREFUL TO DO EVERYTHING WRITTEN IN IT. THEN YOU WILL BE PROSPEROUS AND SUCCESSFUL."

JOSHUA 1:8 NIV

I am faithful with my devotional and prayers in the morning. I have not, however, established an evening routine for prayer and study. This is something that I want to do but seem to have trouble maintaining.

I remember the advice of a pastor to leave my Bible open on my nightstand so that I naturally pick it up before I climb into bed. I think that's a great idea (and I am happy to pass it on), but it hasn't worked for me yet.

A friend gave me a prayer journal with prompts printed on each page. The prompts are things like: "Things I'm grateful for," "Things I'm happy about," "Things I am stressed about," "Who can I help today?" With a little personal tweaking, I think I can adapt this for my evening time with God. It's not a study time but, rather, a conversation. This can be a focused time of prayer and accountability for how I stewarded my time. I think I can maintain this! New goals, new motivation.

I look over the prompts printed in the journal again. The first one says, "Things I am grateful for." I can end my day with thanksgiving and praise to God for what He has done and is doing for me, with me, and through me—every evening.

Today I thank Jesus for my salvation, for my invitation into the family of God and eternity with Him. I am grateful for a video chat with my son and grandson in Florida! I am thankful for technology. I am thankful for good timing and his sweet little boy giggle! I am thankful for the rain. I am thankful for friends (and one in particular today who gifted me the journal). I am thankful for a warm, comfortable, dry home on a damp, cool evening. I am thankful for a pastor and church family. I am thankful for food on the table and in the pantry....Oh, this is just fun!

The next prompt is, "Things I am happy about." I think I will cover that in the gratitude prompt, so I change this one to "Who needs prayer? Who needs Jesus?" One of my pastors challenged the congregation to invite people to church by asking, "Who is close to you but far from God?" That simple statement sticks in my mind. There are so many! Too many. I will write out their names and cover them in prayer. I will lift their names to heaven before I lay my head on the pillow to sleep. I write three precious names tonight.

"Things I am stressed about" comes next in this journal. Stress is a reality of living on this earth. My faith should equip me for facing stressors. I want to follow the prompt with a scripture verse that helps me to respond to the situation. The "Part B" of that prompt will be, "What does God tell me about that?" so that I can meditate on that scripture and hold on to that promise. What will this look like? I am stressed/worried/concerned about moving to a new town, starting a new job. God tells me:

"HAVE I NOT COMMANDED YOU? BE STRONG AND COURAGEOUS. DO NOT BE AFRAID; DO NOT BE DISCOURAGED, FOR THE LORD YOUR GOD WILL BE WITH YOU WHEREVER YOU GO."

JOSHUA 1:9 NIV

The last question is meant for the beginning of the day, so I will change it just a little. Instead of "Who can I help today?" I will write about "Who I helped today." I think this is a fair question for a believer to consider at the end of a day. The fruit of the Spirit is evidence of the Spirit of God in us.

Every day is an opportunity to show love, joy, peace, patience, kindness, goodness, faithfulness, gentleness, or self-control to another human being. I pray that I am able to write my husband's name in my journal here every single evening. So here I go, morning and evening! I'm so excited! How will you challenge yourself?

Reflections

How do you typically spend your evening?

Do you have a morning and an evening prayer routine?

What would you have to give up or change in order to fit in a second time of prayer each day? Do you feel called/motivated to meet God in prayer twice a day?

Preprinted journals can be helpful in guiding our prayer time. Do you like to have a prayer plan or do you prefer a blank page?

I modified the journal prompts to fit my own personality and season. This is what I came up with for evening prayers:

I am grateful for:

People I can pray for:

I am stressed about:

What God's Word says about that:

Who I served today:

As a fully devoted follower of Christ Jesus, what do you want to be held accountable for at the end of each day?

6

❧ · DIGGING DEEP · ❧

CONTEXT: *2 Kings 11–12*

"YOUR WORD IS A LAMP TO GUIDE MY FEET
AND A LIGHT FOR MY PATH." PSALM 119:105

FALL MORNINGS TRANSITIONED quickly from cool to cold this year. It's been in the forties and raining for several days already. It warms up some during the day, but with consistent cloud cover, I'm still reaching for thick socks and my quilted jacket when I go outside.

The ducks let me know they were cold today too. Poppy ran past me when I opened the gate to let my Runners out of their insulated sleeping pen. She waddled three feet beyond the warm enclosure before settling on her belly, lifting her feet off the wet, chilled ground, and tucking them under her wings. This is a winter posture for a duck. Their fat stores are around their bellies. Their leathery webbed feet lack natural protection from the cold. They rest on their tummies and tuck their feet up close to their bodies to warm them. I watched Poppy for a minute to be sure she was just protesting the temperature and nothing else was wrong before I continued my chores.

Fall is the time to prepare for winter. I clean out the electric water buckets that have been in storage for six months. I restock the barn with straw that will provide additional layers of comfort in the coops and barns. The animals, who enjoyed sleeping out under the stars all summer, will come in to the shelters and snuggle close together in the straw for warmth. My husband makes sure we have plenty of firewood—dry, split, stacked, and accessible. There is lots to do in preparation for the coming season that will bring frigid temperatures, ice, and snow.

We work hard to be ready for what storms might come. We know God's Word prepares us for every season of life—for any possible situation we might face. We need to be diligent in preparing our hearts and souls spiritually.

The Holy Spirit is stirring my soul to study hard this season. He is compelling me to open the Bible and look deeper into the Scriptures. I thirst for the things of God like the deer longs for streams of water (Psalm 42). I crave His wisdom and knowing Him more through His Word. It hasn't always been this way for me.

Some seasons, obedience and routine kept me in the Word. Some seasons, I faltered and struggled to open the book. It's not always exciting to read the Scriptures (maybe it's just me?). Why does that happen? I refuse to dwell on the why. Again, I shift my mind to the what. What do I do when the Scriptures seem dry and difficult? What do I do when I catch myself drifting from God's will and His perfect ways?

God's chosen people, His royal priesthood, His holy nation, continually wandered away from Him. I am (and you are) prone to wander. We have to prepare for those dry or bitter cold seasons. We need to stack the firewood of our souls so that it is easy to ignite when the storms blow in. All the answers are in His Word. Yes, really. Yes, always.

I turn to a lesser-known story about a king of Judah, King Joash, as recorded in 2 Kings chapters 11 and 12. I use my study Bible and trusted Internet sites to gather context for the story. King David and King Solomon were strong, faithful, godly leaders. After their deaths, and under the influence of many weak and faithless leaders, Israel was divided into Northern (Israel) and Southern (Judah) kingdoms.

The book of 2 Kings provides details of the downfall and defeat of unfaithful Judah. The story of King Joash is a powerful illustration of the consequences of wandering

from God and His commands—and the influences that breed that heart condition.

Since this is a devotional designed to encourage reflection, and not a true Bible study, I will share three highlights from the story and a few thoughts for meditation. I would encourage you to read 2 Kings 11 and 12 in your own Bible.

Highlight #1:

God is patient, but idolatry always triggers His anger. Joash's life reminds me that we are surrounded by evil, challenges, and choices—all of us, every day.

Consider the commandment God gave first: "You must not have any other god but me" (Exodus 20:3). Idolatry is the common downfall of God's people throughout the Old Testament. Kings and queens of Israel lost sight of God and followed idols until the entire kingdom was defeated and in exile.

Our idols change over the decades and the centuries—but Satan never loses that razor-sharp hook that keeps us distracted and distant from the one true God. Anyone and anything that I worship, prioritize over God in my life, is an idol. What is my idol, my distraction, today? I pause and give it over to God.

A heart postured for divine intervention requires intentionality. I must choose daily whom I will serve (Joshua 24:15). I must be deliberate about "dying to self" in order to be available to what God has to say to me. I must make that choice daily, even moment by moment.

Highlight #2:

God keeps His promises. As an infant, Joash was marked for death by his own grandmother who wanted the crown of Judah for herself. Joash was saved and hidden from Queen Athaliah for years. God promised King David that the Messiah would come through David's royal family.

If Athaliah had been successful in her ambition to kill all the heirs to the throne, she would have wiped out David's line. God protected Joash, and the mighty Lion of Judah did indeed come through Joash and David's royal line.

Highlight #3:

The people with whom we surround ourselves really matter. The people in our environment will influence our hearts, our minds, and our behavior. Early in his reign, young King Joash was influenced by a godly priest, Jehoiada. Under Jehoiada's influence, Joash repaired the temple and honored God. "All his life Joash did what was pleasing in the LORD's sight, because Jehoiada the priest instructed him" (2 Kings 12:2). After his mentor died, Joash was influenced by wicked, idolatrous people. When the prophet Zechariah (who was also Jehoiada's son) warned Joash to change his ways, Joash had Zechariah stoned to death.

Oh, how fast and how far we fall when pride and evil influences have a place in our life. Pride, envy, and selfishness are like daggers to our heart and soul. They shred the work God wants to do in us and through us. No one is immune to this sinful human nature—no one. This is why God gives us a body of believers. Gracious accountability in community keeps us true to His ways!

Because I am in His Word, I am prepared to deal with whatever comes in any season. There is no shortage of lessons to be gleaned from His wisdom and the path of those who walked before us. I rest my pen and let this lesson soak through my tough hide. Thank You, Jesus, that You never give up on me, You never leave me, and You don't even let me wander alone. Keep me close today and every day.

Reflections

Have you read the story of Joash before today?

Which of the three highlights stirred your heart the most, and how:

God is patient.

God keeps His promises.

We are easily influenced by the people around us.

Did you find some highlights of your own in the scriptures?

We can learn so much from the people who went before us when we invest in learning the history. What is your greatest takeaway from the story of Joash?

7

·❧ BIRDS OF A FEATHER ❧·

CONTEXT: *Matthew 6*

"SEEK THE KINGDOM OF GOD ABOVE ALL ELSE,
AND LIVE RIGHTEOUSLY, AND HE WILL GIVE
YOU EVERYTHING YOU NEED." MATTHEW 6:33

I AM A FEATHER-FINDER. You probably just reread that last sentence. I love to find feathers. You might say I'm obsessed with finding feathers. I have nearly a dozen "bouquets" of feathers all around my house. I think they are beautiful.

I have found wing feathers, tail feathers, contour feathers, down feathers, and plume feathers. I have fluffy feathers, straight feathers, spotted feathers, striped feathers, dark feathers, light feathers, colorful feathers, and plain feathers.

I have turkey and pheasant feathers that are over a foot long. I have tiny down feathers that are not an inch long. I have collected feathers on walks in the woods, hikes along trails, in my pasture, and along the canal. If I am outside, I am on the lookout for feathers. I have duck, goose, and chicken feathers. I have turkey, owl, hawk, and pheasant feathers. I have blue bird and blue jay feathers. I have a variety of woodpecker feathers. I have dove feathers, mockingbird feathers, cardinal and wren feathers.

I have feathers I cannot confidently identify, but I still think they are beautiful—so I add them to my bouquet. Before you close this book and give up on me, think of my feather-finding hobby like a stamp-collecting or coin-collecting hobby—or better yet, think about collecting feathers along paths like collecting seashells along a beach. See, it's not so strange now, is it?

I do enjoy finding pretty feathers. Every single found feather provides a tickle of joy reminding me of God's great love of variety and His perfect attention to all of creation. The little bit that I know about the very specific structure and purpose of feathers allows me to appreciate the amazing details in our Creator's design. What an incredible God He is! And how much more, He cares for us.

"LOOK AT THE BIRDS. THEY DON'T PLANT OR HARVEST OR STORE FOOD IN BARNS, FOR YOUR HEAVENLY FATHER FEEDS THEM. AND AREN'T YOU FAR MORE VALUABLE TO HIM THAN THEY ARE? CAN ALL YOUR WORRIES ADD A SINGLE MOMENT TO YOUR LIFE?"

MATTHEW 6:26–27

(Context: This verse in Matthew is part of Jesus' lengthy teaching given on a hillside referred to as the Sermon on the Mount. Jesus spoke to the crowds about how to live a grace-filled life that honors God in this sermon recorded in Matthew chapters 5 to 7.)

"Look at the birds." Okay, I look at those relatively small creatures and I see their beauty. I see the hand of the Creator. I see their majesty in flight. I imagine the peace that comes with soaring among the clouds. I see the seed-eaters and the song birds. I see the nectar-sippers, the predators, and the night owls. I see that each one is a masterpiece of design. I see that they are loved and enjoyed. Thank You, Lord, for this delightful aviator, this song-giver, and this awe-inspiring gift.

"They don't plant or harvest or store food in barns, for your heavenly Father feeds them." I make the spiritual connection. God provides what we need. What He gives is meant to be appreciated, valued, and shared. We are to hold the gifts He gives with a grateful heart and open hand. I think of the contrast of generous living in the parable of the man (called a rich fool) who built bigger barns to hold his surplus supplies—but died before he could ever enjoy what he had (Luke 12:16–21).

I am convinced that God cares about each one of us, in part, through the community in which He places us. I have something to add to the body of Christ—or to someone else in the name of Christ. And so do you. God gives good gifts so that we share what we have with others, in His name.

The scriptures around Matthew 6:26–27 address our attitude toward money and material possessions. God's desire is that we trust that He will provide what we need, that we share what we have, and that we not find security in our possessions.

"SEEK THE KINGDOM OF GOD ABOVE ALL ELSE, AND LIVE RIGHTEOUSLY, AND HE WILL GIVE YOU EVERYTHING YOU NEED."

MATTHEW 6:33

Am I truly doing that? I copy the verse. I underline "need." I circle the phrase "he will give you everything you need." I draw an arched arrow from the circled phrase to the beginning of the sentence, "Seek the Kingdom of God." I underline "above all else." I circle "all." I read the verse again with all my squiggles and lines.

Am I committed to using my time, talent, and resources all for Him, and for the people He loves. Is my security in His provision or in my abilities? I pause here. I remind myself—it's not about me.

Can all your worries add a single moment to your life? It's crazy how much damage worry and anxiety can cause. The consequences of stress on our mental, physical, and spiritual health are well known. The scripture tells me "worry will not add a single moment to my life"—but I know from experience that worry will surely poison far more than a moment of my life, if I allow it.

When I worry about something, then I'm probably not trusting God completely. Am I giving more power to the Enemy than to the plan of God? Am I focused on what I can do—or what God can do? Or maybe, I have an agenda or a desired outcome? To live fully submitted to the work and power of God in my life, I must let go of what I want—even what I understand sometimes. That's not easy to do.

Not for an independent girl like me. It rubs against my grain to surrender. I need Your help with this, Lord Jesus.

I imagine worry as a poison to my heart, constricting the muscle until the beat slows and stops. I see anxiety for the thief that it is—stealing my joy and suffocating my spirit. I see the potion in the Enemy's hand and I decline to accept it. Not today, not ever.

Gracious heavenly Father, I don't always understand what You are doing in the moment—but I do trust Your unfailing love, Your kind mercy, and Your perfect plan. Help me to be a loyal steward of all that You have provided. I praise You for welcoming me into the body of Christ and for the friends and family that surround me with love, support, and encouragement.

Reflections

Many of the verses in Matthew 6 talk about doing things for the Lord in private, not publicly for all to see. Jesus is directing us to a humble heart posture. Social media is all about living out loud. Social media platforms exist to show everyone who we are and what we do. How is this a challenge for a Christ-follower?

Material possessions and working to achieve them can become our idols (Matthew 6:24). The pursuit of "nice things" can capture our hearts, our time, and our attention. Is this a challenge for you? Why or why not?

Look again at Matthew 6:31–33. Matthew is telling us there is a difference in how a believer thinks (worries). Do these verses challenge you at all? Why or why not?

8

CONTEXT: *Philippians 1:1-11*

"AND I AM CERTAIN THAT GOD, WHO BEGAN THE GOOD WORK WITHIN YOU, WILL CONTINUE HIS WORK UNTIL IT IS FINALLY FINISHED ON THE DAY WHEN CHRIST JESUS RETURNS." PHILIPPIANS 1:6

THE REMNANTS OF a late season hurricane came up through the Mid-Atlantic states this week. The storm brought four days of rain to western Maryland. Goats do not like the rain. They stayed in their shelters for the better part of the week. The ducks, on the other hand, enjoyed splashing and foraging in the puddles. They celebrated the gift of earthworms breaking the surface of the soil in the soaking rains. They quacked, honked, and flapped their wings joyfully while dining on extra portions of the wiggly snacks.

Inside the house, we have two senior and one young, energetic dog. The oldest dog came home with me thirteen years ago from a shelter visit. The other two dogs are "foster fail" dogs. A "foster fail" is a rescue dog adopted by their foster parents. Let me just say that my husband has revoked my right to visit shelters and to foster dogs.

Roxie and Abbey, my senior pups, are content to sleep through a storm—even one that lasts four days. Ava, my two-year-old, thirty-pound terrier mix, is not. Ava typically joins me for a five-mile walk, hike, or run-walk several days a week. Four days of pacing inside made us both a little crazy. The sun finally broke through the clouds today and Ava and I made a break for the canal (our favorite walk-run path).

Ava knows the path. She loves the trail. She will alter her pace but not her direction. She knows the turnaround point. She knows when we are close to home. Ava does not like to change her course. She is fully committed to the way she knows and will plant her feet firmly in protest to any hint of off-roading or suggestion of side trails.

The path was muddy today, as you might imagine after four days of rain. I steered Ava around the puddles. She was content with puddle jumping as long as we stayed on the designated path. At one point, I pulled Ava's leash to leave the wet canal path and take a dry, paved side road. I pulled. Ava sat. I coaxed. Ava looked away. I bribed her with a treat. Ava said, "No way."

I picked her up and carried her a little way on the dry road. Ava whined and looked over my shoulder. When I finally put her down and began to jog again, she came along reluctantly. She glanced at me while we ran, with a look that said, "I hope you know where you are going."

Back home, I reflect on our brief adventure. Does Ava need to relax and be more adventurous—or do I need to be more like Ava, convicted in direction and committed to my course? I ponder this while I open my study Bible.

I choose Philippians, the book of joy. These pages are saturated in translucent yellow and blue highlighter ink. Words and phrases are circled. Arrows, stars, and notes fill the margins. This is the book that reminds me that God isn't finished with me yet—and that He is fully committed to my spiritual development (Philippians 1:6). This book encourages me to have the humble heart and mind of Christ as He made the most humble sacrifice of all (Philippians 2:3–8). This book calls me to focus on things that are worthy of our attention (Philippians 4:8) and the eternal prize (Philippians 3:20–21).

My eyes rest on the yellow highlights and pink circles that cover Philippians 1:9–11. I copy the verses, a prayer

written by the apostle Paul, from the New Living Translation into my journal.

> "I PRAY THAT YOUR LOVE WILL OVERFLOW MORE AND MORE, AND THAT YOU WILL KEEP ON GROWING IN KNOWLEDGE AND UNDERSTANDING. FOR I WANT YOU TO UNDERSTAND WHAT REALLY MATTERS, SO THAT YOU MAY LIVE PURE AND BLAMELESS LIVES UNTIL THE DAY OF CHRIST'S RETURN. MAY YOU ALWAYS BE FILLED WITH THE FRUIT OF YOUR SALVATION—THE RIGHTEOUS CHARACTER PRODUCED IN YOUR LIFE BY JESUS CHRIST— FOR THIS WILL BRING MUCH GLORY AND PRAISE TO GOD."

I ask the Holy Spirit to move me to a greater depth of understanding now as I revisit these scriptures. I pause for prayer before I pick up my colored pens and my commentary.

What caught my attention the last time I read this section of scripture was the end of verse 9: "keep on growing in knowledge and understanding." Brilliant yellow ink glows over the words on the tissue-thin Bible paper. This time, a different verse—verse 11, "the fruit of your salvation"— rises from the page and keeps my attention. This is what reading the living, breathing Word of God is. Words and phrases viewed in black and white take on transformational power with insight. As truth is revealed, my heart beats faster. The Holy Spirit is the whisper that says, "Stay here with me."

The fruit of my salvation...

Spiritual fruit is evidence, the natural product, of our faith. It is who we are and what we do in partnership with Jesus Christ. A transformed life bears spiritual fruit, period. Galatians 5:22–23 lists the fruit of the Spirit: love, joy, peace, patience, kindness, goodness, faithfulness, gentleness, and self-control. These are not just pleasant character qualities; they describe the authentic heart and soul of a believer—they allow us to reflect Jesus Christ to the world!

I use the lexicon to look at the original text. The word "salvation" in the NLT is transcribed from the Greek word *dikaisone*.[13] I notice that other Bible translations use the word "righteousness" instead of "salvation." Righteousness in this context refers to the verdict of God's approval, which is received through our salvation in Jesus. I like the decision to use the word "salvation" here. I appreciate the clarity. Jesus saves us and so we bear fruit—we reflect Him, serve Him, and bear witness to Him through our life well-lived. God equips us to serve Him in many ways, but a significant part of "equipping" is growing our character in Christlikeness. Staying the course allows the Holy Spirit to do this transforming work over a lifetime.

Paul finished his prayer by reminding us that the power of a life lived according to God's righteousness is a life that "will bring much glory and praise to God." This is the call to every believer—to point the way to God's family through the saving work of Jesus. We point the way to His love and grace when we consistently overflow with the love He pours in. Consistently, faithfully, steadily on course.

While the world goes sideways, I will keep my focus straight ahead. I want to be someone who brings hope and light in a world that is growing increasingly dark. Jesus, prepare me for that task. Thank You for Your Word that keeps me on the path of truth and integrity, of hope, love, and mercy. Allow me to be an encouragement to others and a witness for You along the way.

---

13 James Strong, *The New Strong's Expanded Exhaustive Concordance of the Bible*, Red letter ed. (Nashville: Thomas Nelson, 2010, 1343.

Reflections

Are you an adventurer and explorer by nature—or do you tend to follow a well-worn path?

Write Philippians 1:9–11 in your own journal and meditate on the words. What is the Spirit saying to you today? What words or phrases call your highlighter?

The fruit of the Spirit (Galatians 5:22–23) is evidence of the Holy Spirit at work in us. As you review the list, do you find any that you need to develop/mature? God is committed to our spiritual development. He absolutely will help you!

LOVE, JOY, PEACE, PATIENCE, KINDNESS, GOODNESS, FAITHFULNESS, GENTLENESS, SELF-CONTROL

Listen to "He Who Began a Good Work in You" while you color the next page.

9

SOMETIMES THEY STING · PART ONE · ᐖ

CONTEXT: *Luke 6:27-32*

"BUT TO YOU WHO ARE WILLING TO LISTEN, I SAY,
LOVE YOUR ENEMIES! DO GOOD TO THOSE WHO
HATE YOU. BLESS THOSE WHO CURSE YOU. PRAY
FOR THOSE WHO HURT YOU." LUKE 6:27-28

———

I'd put it off long enough. It was time to pull weeds and fading summer flowers out of the front garden. Maybe I could even get my fall decorations out. It was a clear, cool Saturday morning and a perfect day for outdoor chores.

That was the plan—a pleasant morning in the garden and then some festive seasonal decorating. As often as is the case, things did not go according to plan. I didn't get very far into the flower pulling when I disturbed the nest of some very angry yellow jacket wasps. Before I even realized that I dug into their underground home, they were stinging me. It happened so unexpectedly. Sharp pricks followed by instant heat and pain registered in my body and in my brain.

I swatted at the swarm of ill-tempered insects and ran for the house. Yellow jackets are quick and fierce. They are the type of insect I would normally do my best to avoid. My granddaughter's preschool voice echoed in my mind and I heard her say, "You mean" (her favorite pout when she doesn't get her way).

Standing at the sink rubbing ice cubes over my battle wounds, I rethink my plans. My hand is throbbing and my neck is itching from the stings. I am not happy about it—but I can't go back to the one chore that I hoped to accomplish today. It will take hours for those wasps to settle down. I decide to clean the goat pens instead.

By the end of the day, I have completed several chores, spent time with the animals, helped my husband with some tasks, and made a nice dinner. When my husband prays over the meal, I add a silent thanks for not being allergic to yellow jacket venom.

I've been thinking a lot about godly character in general and God's plan for me in particular. It hasn't been a simple transformation from my old ways of thinking, reacting, and behaving—to God's ways. As a new believer, I had as much unlearning to do as I had knowledge to obtain. The Holy Spirit has His hands full with me. Over this lifetime of hard lessons in peace and patience, in mercy and compassion, in humility and forgiveness, my heart has completely changed. I am so thankful. I know that there is more to learn and (always) more room to grow.

He is stirring my heart again. Recently, He has raised the theme of loving difficult and unlovable people like a flag to get my attention. It started with a vague awareness in the back of my mind and grew in focus, frequency, and intensity over the past several weeks. This command now fills the space in my thoughts, time in my prayers, and opportunities to practice. "Love your enemies" are not new words to me, but they are now part of God's personal assignment for me. I am listening. My spirit and my heart are leaning in to hear. It's the difference between knowing on the surface of your brain and understanding/accepting with your whole being.

Like those unlikable yellow jackets, some people sting. I don't like prickly people and I tend to avoid them. While I cannot discount the value of healthy boundaries in toxic relationships, sometimes, maybe "boundaries" have become my excuse to ignore people who God loves and I can serve.

Is this the next hard lesson for developing my character to Christlikeness, God's plan for me? If loving difficult people is not part of my character, then I am not reflecting Jesus. I do believe that this is something that I have side-stepped in the past. It's a practice that we can easily justify and excuse—at least I did. The Holy Spirit is calling me to address it now.

I start my study from my computer. I use my search engine to look for verses that speak about loving difficult people. There are nearly one hundred to review. There are two that shout to me above the rest:

"DEAR FRIENDS, LET US CONTINUE TO LOVE ONE ANOTHER, FOR LOVE COMES FROM GOD. ANYONE WHO LOVES IS A CHILD OF GOD AND KNOWS GOD. BUT ANYONE WHO DOES NOT LOVE DOES NOT KNOW GOD, FOR GOD IS LOVE... AND AS WE LIVE IN GOD, OUR LOVE GROWS MORE PERFECT."

1 JOHN 4:7-8, 17

"BUT TO YOU WHO ARE WILLING TO LISTEN, I SAY, LOVE YOUR ENEMIES! DO GOOD TO THOSE WHO HATE YOU. BLESS THOSE WHO CURSE YOU. PRAY FOR THOSE WHO HURT YOU. ... IF YOU LOVE ONLY THOSE WHO LOVE YOU, WHY SHOULD YOU GET

CREDIT FOR THAT? EVEN SINNERS LOVE THOSE WHO LOVE THEM!"

LUKE 6:27-28, 32

It isn't natural to love someone who is unkind or even hurtful toward us. Natural human responses to an adversary would be avoidance, defensiveness, confrontation, or even revenge—whether in thought or deed. It is supernatural to respond to an offender with grace, mercy, kindness, and love. God expects the supernatural response because He is love. And because He is in us. When we yield our spirit to His, He makes the impossible possible.

I have experienced this many times in a familiar context. The Holy Spirit gives me an unexplainable love for the women who attend my Bible studies. As soon as they enter my home and join our little study group, I am overwhelmed with Christ's love for them. He does this when I teach the children at church. He gives me a love for even the most difficult child under my care. I am convinced that this is an extension of the spiritual gift given to His teachers and shepherds. This is truly the work of the Holy Spirit. I feel it. I know it.

However, I'm not consistent with yielding. In my immaturity, I surrender to God in some situations but not all. I pause now to pray. His Spirit mingles with mine as I meditate over the truth of His Word and the weakness of my heart. Memories of the pain that accompanied divine interventions in the past rise to the surface. I feel alert and wary. I know how challenges bring about a change of heart and mind that cannot be received any other way—but I also know that most of those challenges sting.

Like a small child warned not to touch the stove because it's hot, I want to back away. But He is compelling me forward. I pick up my pen and draw a silhouette of a cross on the page in front of me. I draw a heart in the center of the cross. I pause again as His Spirit envelops me with peace. I pick up my red coloring pencil and start to color in the cross.

Cruciform means made in the image of the cross. I imagine the cross on my heart. Jesus' life for mine. My pencil stops. I have nothing to offer to our perfect, loving, holy God but myself. I surrender another piece of control. *Help my life to "cruciform" for You, Jesus. I trust You to bring me through another challenge, to grow my roots a little deeper, to bring me still closer to who You know I am. I am Yours.*

Stay in this moment of quiet reflection with me. Ask the Spirit of God to examine your heart. Pray for awareness. What is God saying to you about love? Let's meet again tomorrow as we finish this thought.

Reflections

God is showing me that I need to grow in the area of forgiveness and in loving difficult people? I think this is hard for many people but Jesus asks us to do hard things sometimes. How do you do around difficult people, unlovely people?

What strategies do you use when challenged by an unkind or unloving person?

What scripture verses remind you of God's expectations that we should love one another?

Healthy boundaries are important but not necessarily perma-nent. Ask God to help you to discern if, when and how to ease (or to erect) boundaries. Revisiting boundaries can help us move toward another step in our spiritual growth.

10

SOMETIMES THEY STING · PART TWO · ⌇

CONTEXT: *Acts 9:1-19*

"NOW THERE WAS A BELIEVER IN DAMASCUS
NAMED ANANIAS. THE LORD SPOKE TO
HIM IN A VISION, CALLING, 'ANANIAS!'

'YES, LORD!' HE REPLIED." ACTS 9:10

THE HOLY SPIRIT can reach us with a hint, a whisper, or the smallest of thoughts. He can also roar so that His call is unmistakable. I walked into our Sunday morning church service today and heard His mighty roar, that resounding voice of divine certainty. Our pastor introduced the sermon. He was teaching from 1 Samuel 24 about how the Lord led David to show respect and honor to his enemy, King Saul. David bowed down in homage to a sin-sick man that wanted to kill him. Only God can do this kind of work. This is the life of a believer that the world does not, and cannot, understand.

God's plan seems perfectly clear to me. *It's time to learn to love your enemies, Deborah.*

I can't say that I am bracing myself for what is coming, because I trust Him. I am, however, certain that this next season will be a powerful spiritual season as long as I remain surrendered and obedient to the work He wants to do in me and through me.

I am equally certain that this will only be achieved through the work that God initiates and the Spirit leads. Loving like Jesus is not achieved by willpower, but only by *His* power.

The story of Saul and Ananias (recorded in Acts 9:1–19) is another picture, a New Testament teaching, of following God's command to love our enemies. It may be a familiar story but worth the time to review. It is the story of Saul's miraculous conversion from zealous hunter and killer of Jesus' disciples to becoming a believer himself. Open your Bible to this passage now and read it before you continue.

Consider the context. The number of believers (also called followers of the Lord, followers of the Way, or disciples) increased following the death and resurrection of Christ and the coming of the Holy Spirit at Pentecost. The antagonism of the Jewish leaders for the followers of Jesus did not diminish. Saul was a Jewish leader who hated Jesus' disciples. He threatened, imprisoned, and killed Christians. Acts 9:1 says that Saul was "eager to kill the Lord's followers." Saul was a well-known, much-feared adversary of all believers.

Scripture tells us Saul was traveling to Damascus to arrest disciples. "He wanted to bring them—both men and women—back to Jerusalem in chains" (v. 2). Saul was responsible for separating families and torturing and stoning people to death. Hatred and anger coursed through his proud veins. His arrogance quelled any possibility of empathy or remorse. I imagine this is the kind of enmity anyone would wrestle with in the aftermath of a tragic loss to violence. How do you forgive someone who causes this much harm, this much grief? This was Saul. Killer of families. Notorious, shameless persecutor of believers.

I continue my reading. Saul was blinded when he encountered Jesus on the road to Damascus. He had to be led by the hand to town. He remained blind and helpless for three days.

How would I feel if my tormentor was rendered vulnerable or weak? I think I would feel relief, maybe even satisfaction. Perhaps I would think justice was served.

I read further.

Verse 10 tells us that the Lord spoke to Ananias—a follower of Jesus, a target of Saul's chains and violence—and asked Ananias to help his enemy, Saul. I want to share what I see in this conversation between Ananias and the Lord.

I see a beloved and obedient disciple.

I see loving obedience in the immediate and affirming way Ananias responded to being called: "Yes, Lord!" he replied (v. 10). I hear the excitement in his voice and I have to believe that God was pleased with Ananias's prompt yes.

I see a healthy, respectful, honest relationship.

The Lord gave Ananias very specific instructions in verses 11 and 12. Ananias was afraid. He told the Lord what he knew about Saul and that Saul was doing terrible things to believers. Ananias shared his heart, a heart of concern. He wasn't rebelling or refusing to go—he was afraid to go. The Lord responded to Ananias's heart and explained the purpose of Ananias's visit to Saul (vv. 15–16).

I see an emboldened follower who trusts God's plan.

"So Ananias went and found Saul" (v. 17). With a clear sense of purpose to the grander cause of sharing the good news, Ananias followed the instructions given by the Lord. He wasn't told that he would be safe—he was only told that Jesus would use Saul to spread the gospel message to the Gentiles and others. Ananias was a fully devoted follower committed to God's plan and purpose.

I've read more than a hundred Bible verses about the love of God and the command to love others, even our enemies, over the last several days. There is no getting around it. No more excuses. I don't have a "Saul" in my life at the moment and I really don't want one. I do, however, have difficult people, prickly people, unlovely people, and people who will no doubt "sting" when I reach out in my life.

I want to be like Ananias. I want to follow God's commands with holy boldness. I don't want "Christian" to be my label or my club. I want it to be my lifestyle. I want my heart conformed—*cruciformed*—with my life, reflecting Jesus in all that I do. I know, even as I ask this in prayer, that God will give me the opportunity to practice and grow in this area. *Lord, I need You, I know I do. Help me to love well, even my enemies.*

Reflections

Loving our enemies is one of those hard things Jesus asks us to do—because He did that for us. We were enemies of God in our sin when Jesus died for us. How does this perspective help you to love your enemies?

Consider the three traits I saw in Ananias. Do you see yourself in any of them? Which one do you wish you saw more of in yourself?

1) obedient disciple

2) honest relationship with Jesus

3) trusts God's plan

Ananias responded with faith. I assume he was still afraid, but he did what Jesus instructed. Can you relate to his choice to obey? Why or why not?

I am convinced that only the power of God in me will allow me to love my enemies. What do you think?

11

CONTEXT: *1 Corinthians 1:26-30*

"REMEMBER, DEAR BROTHERS AND SISTERS,
THAT FEW OF YOU WERE WISE IN THE WORLD'S
EYES OR POWERFUL OR WEALTHY WHEN
GOD CALLED YOU." 1 CORINTHIANS 1:26

SHEPHERD'S GATE FARM is a small hobby farm. We raise and grow just enough for our family and a little extra to share. We have a baker's dozen count of dairy goats, a few ounces of chickens, and a dash of ducks. Our largest animal is our 150-pound dog-bear who bravely guards our precious herd.

As long as I can remember, I've been drawn to small numbers, tiny sizes, and wee creatures. It may have something to do with my own diminutive stature—or it may just be how God gets my attention. He shows me the beauty in humility and the power of a small-scale focus. "Small" is not equivalent to "inconsequential." God's plans are, more often than not, the antithesis of our worldly expectations.

God birthed His beloved nation from a couple "too old" to produce children (Abraham and Sarah). God employed one senior shepherd to lead millions out of slavery (Moses). God saw a small boy as a mighty, faithful king (David).

God used one small stone to kill a fearsome giant (Goliath). God turned a single serving of bread and fish into a feast to feed thousands.

There are so many more examples that point to God's heart for using the small, the weak, and the powerless—things that seem insignificant and foolish to us—to change the course of history, to expand His kingdom on earth, and to demonstrate His omnipotent glory.

"GOD CHOSE THINGS DESPISED BY THE WORLD, THINGS COUNTED AS NOTHING AT ALL, AND USED THEM TO BRING NOTHING WHAT THE WORLD CONSIDERS IMPORTANT."

1 CORINTHIANS 1:28

"THEREFORE, AS THE SCRIPTURES SAY, 'IF YOU WANT TO BOAST, BOAST ONLY ABOUT THE LORD.'"

1 CORINTHIANS 1:31

What can I offer up to God in praise and in sacrifice to Him today, trusting that He can do mighty things with my meager offering?

What "small stone" will He use to slay a monster—when I offer it with a pure heart of obedience?

If you can relate to what I share, look up and copy the Bible reference provided. Alternatively, work on your own list and references. What small things can you offer back to God to use in a powerful way today?

He has given me a voice to share my love for Him. I use that voice in my writing, teaching, and artwork within my community. I use my voice in cards of encouragement, text messages, and emails to family and friends. I use my voice to support fellow believers and creative worship artists in their efforts to reach and teach. I use my voice to build the body of Christ as the Spirit leads me everywhere I go. This small voice can speak volumes of life and love to others. *Use my voice, my pen, my paintbrush for your glory, dear Jesus. Thank You, Lord.* (1 Peter 4:10)

He has given me a farm—land and animals and a beautiful environment to care for and to share with others.

I open my heart through my home for Bible studies, celebrations, meals, fellowship opportunities, children's activities, and family events. This humble home has been shared with hundreds of people. *Use our home, our land, our space, dear Jesus, for Your honor and glory. Thank You, Lord.* (Romans 12:13)

He has given me time.

Oh how He has grown my heart and mind over the decades. I am not the same person I was five, ten, and twenty years ago. I am so very grateful for the gift of time to grow my roots deep and to be transformed ever closer to Jesus. I am willing to invest my time into others—to share, to mentor, to lift up the younger generations as they live out their own faith and struggle (as I did!) along the way. We are never alone in our faith journey. *Use me to embrace, lead, mentor, and lift humble, hungry hearts for Your glory. Thank You, Lord.* (1 Peter 5:2)

He has given me a healthy body.

I love to be outside and moving. I love to run and walk and hike and paddle! Outdoors in my happy place. As I make every effort to keep this earthly body strong and healthy, I am available to offer physical assistance to others. I am available in mind and body to support and help. I have strength to care for the land and the animals, to prepare meals and deliver them, to walk and talk for hours. I am so thankful that I can still move comfortably. *Use these willing hands and feet for Your glory, dear Jesus. Thank You, Lord.* (Psalm 139:13)

He granted me patience and stillness.

This is a gift I use daily now. He shows me that quiet waiting and steady attention is a blessing of love to others. I wasn't capable of this in my youth. I was too eager, too impulsive, and too insensitive to see the beauty of a slow and gentle pace. God broke my pride to show me my foolish, selfish attitude. Pain yields strength. His power is often found in the quiet waiting. *Help me to spread the gift of patience for Your glory. Thank You, Lord.* (Romans 12:12)

He has given me a passion to encourage others.

I simply follow His lead here. I don't even think about it really. I respond automatically to the opportunities He brings for me to support and love. This is something that flows naturally from the abundance that He pours in. He loves, so I love. He provides, so I provide. *Thank You, Lord.* (1 Thessalonians 5:11)

He has given me the written Word to read, to learn, to share.

What a gift the Scriptures are! The more I pore over the treasure, the more gold and pearls I have to share. Trust grows with love, and obedience comes easily in a love relationship. *Your Word is sustenance, the nourishment our souls crave. You draw us in and grow us up through the study of Your Word. Use me to lead others in study and devotions, always pointing someone ever closer to You. Thank You, Lord.* (2 Timothy 3:16–17)

I am so grateful for every opportunity to share Your glory! Amen.

Reflections

We cannot wait to be perfect or powerful or influential or popular before we share our gifts and resources. In fact, if I understand the Scriptures correctly, Jesus isn't interested in any of the things the world thinks are important. He is interested in watching what we do with what He has provided! He is a proud Papa waiting for us to take our first steps into ministry and reach out to others!

What "small" things has God given you, and how can you use them for His glory today? Make your own list.

Can you find scriptures that support your gifts?

Enjoy "King of My Heart" as you color the next page and reflect on God's good gifts to us.

12

✤· ONE LAP AROUND THE SUN ·✤

CONTEXT: *Joshua 1:8-9*

"THIS IS MY COMMAND—BE STRONG AND
COURAGEOUS! DO NOT BE AFRAID OR
DISCOURAGED. FOR THE LORD YOUR GOD IS
WITH YOU WHEREVER YOU GO." JOSHUA 1:8-9

WE MADE IT! We finished one lap around the sun together. We shared four seasons together. I am so grateful for every minute. I pray that you feel more confident in the different ways to study His Word and soak in His Presence than when we started. There are so many great teachers and published studies available to choose from these days, but don't neglect your own quiet time with Him, alone in His Word without anyone else's suggestions. That is precious time when He grows your personal relationship and calls to you uniquely.

The last thing I want to share with you from my reflections is the life verse God gave me in the early days of our relationship:

This is my command—be strong and courageous! Do not be afraid or discouraged. For the LORD your God is with you wherever you go." (Joshua 1:9)

This scripture has lifted me through every challenge and motivated me to remain faithful through every endeavor over the last thirty years. My twenties, thirties, and forties were marked by tremendous upheaval—changes in physical location, career, spiritual and emotional focus, even churches. There was little stability or continuity during those seasons of my life.

To be honest, I embraced change like a bull that stepped into a hornets' nest. To say that I dislike changing my routine or space is a ridiculous understatement. I don't know about you, but I like to build my "nest" and stay put. I like to control my environment and my schedule. Routine and control were the source of comfort and safety. It was a part of my nature—a character weakness—that God needed to shift so that I could learn to depend on Him.

God brought that single, simple, beautiful verse when I was twenty-something, before I had even read the book of Joshua. I didn't know Joshua's life or story—but this verse was repeated in multiple contexts by different people over a period of a few days. The verse showed up first in my morning devotional. As I was running errands later that day with my car tuned to the local Christian radio station, the announcer read the day's memory verse: Joshua 1:9. The next day, the verse found me through an email from a friend. Over and over, this verse "appeared." God got my attention and I memorized the verse.

Joshua 1:9 became the warm blanket of God's love that covered me through every change. This verse brought me back to the truth that I was never alone in any struggle or challenge. God was able to draw me in and grow me up with every transition until I truly did welcome change—because I was confident that He would be with me and that He would teach me something significant through it. He molded me slowly and patiently as I yielded in His hands.

Can I be embarrassingly honest here? For all those decades that I relied on Joshua 1:9 for comfort, it was only recently that I considered the verse right before it. It's been easy to find cards, key rings, and even jewelry with Joshua 1:9 etched on them. Apparently, it is an encouraging scripture verse for many. But I've never seen a piece of home decor or pretty bauble with Joshua 1:8 etched on it. Look at that verse with me:

"Study this Book of Instruction continually. Meditate on it day and night so you will be sure to obey everything written in it. Only then will you prosper and succeed in all you do."

Oh, how our gracious heavenly Father grows us up—if we let Him. This verse would not have penetrated my prideful, independent, immature, twentysomething-year-old heart—but oh how it makes my spirit sing today!

Years of living and learning, sacrifice and surrender, pain and brokenness, yield joy in His Presence! His love for us pours out through His Word. There is no better way to experience God Himself than through His Word.

"Only then" stands out on the page to me. Verses 8 and 9 go together. God makes our way (our course of life) successful (moves us forward) as we study and obey His commands. Strength and courage come through knowing God, trusting Him, and living according to God's laws (His ways and precepts that we learn by reading His Word). Verse 9 is the result of verse 8. I put them together now and see the power of His Word. Do you see it? Does it make your heart pound as it does mine?

My friend, I pray for you today. I pray that you will fall in love—maybe for the first time, or maybe all over again—with this powerful Book, with the Hand that authored it, with the Spirit that illuminates it. Wherever you are in your life journey, seek Him first. Seek Him, the Creator, the Gift Giver, the Lover of our soul. Just Him. Let everything else fall away while you spend time with the One who loves you completely. Let the teaching of trusted pastors and teachers build your knowledge, but always, always seek fervently for that time alone with Him and His Word to grow you personally.

Thank you for sharing this year with me, dear reader. May you be blessed with peace and courage and passion to lean hard on Him in this coming year.

Blessings,
Deborah

"YOU WILL KEEP IN PERFECT PEACE
ALL WHO TRUST IN YOU, ALL WHOSE
THOUGHTS ARE FIXED ON YOU."

ISAIAH 26:3

Meet Deborah

DEBORAH HALL SUBETTO holds a master's degree in speech and hearing science from The Ohio State University in Columbus, Ohio. With a remarkable career spanning almost three decades as a speech-language pathologist, she dedicated herself to helping others communicate more effectively. However, when Deborah felt the calling of God in her life, she embraced a new purpose: spreading the gospel through her writing, leading women's Bible studies, and sharing her insightful farm experiences with children and adults alike. Her unwavering passion for God's Word, devotion to family, commitment to mentoring others, fervent expression of her faith, and deep affection for her cherished animals define her.

Deborah Hall Subetto runs her farm with her husband, Jay, in Hagerstown, Maryland. She is a frequent speaker at women's events and has a charming devotional podcast designed to give listeners a quick Biblical and inspirational jumpstart to their day. Find her podcast on Spotify through the QR code below and follow her on social media to know when new books, podcasts, or events are available:

Facebook: facebook.com/deborahhallsubetto

Instagram: instagram.com/deborah_hall_subetto/

Website: shepherdsgatefarm.biz

To inquire about speaking or to schedule an interview, contact Deborah directly at: sgfarm2011@gmail.com

Spotify podcast

Love Notes from Shepherd's Gate Farm, first in the series, offers a fresh, intimate look at creation through Deborah's eyes as she tends to her Maryland farm. Filled with unique glimpses into farm life, this light and joyful seasonal devotional is a collection of thoughtful, sometimes personal, observations that illustrate biblical truths through stories of taking care of her animals and the farm itself.

Lessons from Shepherd's Gate Farm is a continuation from Subetto's first book, with captivating and insightful devotions that take the reader deeper in their faith as they imagine themselves being part of the bucolic life on Shepherd's Gate Farm.

Reflections from Shepherd's Gate Farm is third in Deborah's series of devotionals, each one taking the reader deeper into study and application of God's Word. Reflections is a unique, larger format devotion that includes original artwork designed to help the reader make a creative connection to the stories and biblical application, and provides a spacious landscape and other prompts, examples, and encouragement for the reader to interact with the text as they progress. Intended to be read alongside your Bible with art supplies and colored pens and pencils in hand, Reflections is created to be an engaging, joyful, and thought-provoking pathway to a deeper relationship with God.

All of Deborah's books are available through the author, the publisher, or your favorite bookstore, online or in-person.

Subscribe at www.encouragepublishing.com to be notified of Deborah's wonderful upcoming releases.

CHILDREN'S BOOKS BY DEBORAH HALL SUBETTO

ROOTED IN THE KING'S GARDEN, the first volume in the "Your Child and You" series, is a two-book set that includes a book for your child and one for you, based on the fruit of the Spirit.

A full-color children's story and activity book with dozens of games, puzzles, coloring pages, and more will help you have meaningful and appropriate gospel conversations with your younger children or grandchildren.

A shepherd's edition just for you, with companion activities for you to enjoy alongside your child, includes a devotion for each segment designed for your own growth and encouragement. This truly engaging and innovative book set comes with a beautiful playlist to help you bring meaningful music into your time together.

PERFECT FOR HOMESCHOOL, SUNDAY SCHOOL, VBS, AND MOPS!

VIOLET ASKS - WHAT IS EASTER FOR? and VIOLET ASKS - WHAT IS CHRISTMAS FOR, Volumes 2 and 3 in the "Your Child and You" series, are just right for young children, providing a colorful, beautifully illustrated series of poems that help connect our holiday traditions to the true meaning of each season. In the back of each book find a fun recipe to make together with your little, and some easy conversation starters to help you have those all-important gospel conversations - right on their level.

If you are a church, reseller, or nonprofit interested in ordering multiple copies of any of Deborah Hall Subetto's titles, contact the publisher directly (info@encouragebooks.com) for bulk rate savings or order through Ingram or Spring Arbor.

THE REFLECTIONS TEAM

Reflections from Shepherd's Gate Farm is the product of a team of dedicated professionals for whom we are extremely grateful and wish to give credit:

Author and Illustrator: Deborah Hall Subetto

Cover and interior design: Karol Bailey

Developmental edit: Leslie Turner and Molly Turner

Copy edit: Lisa Grimenstein

Cover photography: Jake Taylor, JT Photography

Author photography: Katelyn Watson

Interior photography: Deborah Hall Subetto

Encourage Publishing has multiple imprints, including Encourage Books, Encourage Music, Encourage Kids, Wildfly, Turner Creative, and Alienta! Learn more about Encourage Publishing, our titles, and our submission requirements at encouragepublishing.com.

Encourage Publishing
(812) 987-6148
info@encouragebooks.com
www.encouragepublishing.com

Thank you

Your reviews online are invaluable, but Deborah would also deeply appreciate your direct feedback. Her hope for *Reflections* was that adults who wanted to go deeper with the Lord in their time alone with Him would find an engaging and strong tool in *Reflections* along with some personal encouragement and enjoyment for themselves. Would you like to see more? What would you like to see done differently? Where are you in life, and what challenges do you face?

To send your feedback to Deborah directly, or to invite her to speak or make an appearance at your event or location, please contact her at sgfarm2011@gmail.com.

You may also send this feedback to her through her publisher at info@encouragebooks.com.

And, if you would like to leave an honest review, please find Reflections on Amazon, Christianbook.com, or your favorite review site.